Advance Praise for
FAME SHARK

"Royal Young's memoir is about a dreamer, set in the post-apocalyptic celebrity world of today. Young, who grew up in New York—like Holden Caulfield, if he wanted to be famous—is looking for adventure and action, and becomes entangled in all sorts of romantic and sordid relationships. He points out the perplexing tragedy (and good fortune, I think) of what it means to be talented and rebellious, but not a celebrity."

—Lily Koppel, bestselling author of *The Astronaut Wives Club* and *The Red Leather Diary*

"Fame Shark is *American Psycho* meets *Call It Sleep*. A no-holds -barred saga of the extremes a human being can go to in his or her quest for attention. Young has the precocity and audacity of Shelley and the fearlessness of Philippe Petit."

—Francis Levy, author of *Erotomania: A Romance* and *Seven Days in Rio*

"Courageously confessional ... Royal Young's searing emotions burst through the page. At times I read *Fame Shark* through tears."

— Jaime Lubin, *The Huffington Post*

"They often say New Yorkers aren't actually from here, but Royal is that rare aborigine who grew up in the Lower East Side and knows that area in ways the rest of us never will. For most of us, New York is an ambition. For Royal, it's a fact of everyday life to be among artists and drug addicts and schemers and all those shady and beautiful people the rest of us move to The City to live among. Read it for the flash and the stories, but also for a sense of the New York that is (already) fast disappearing."

—Meakin Armstrong, Senior Editor/Fiction Editor, *Guernica*

"Shameless, elegant, obscene."
—Leopoldine Core, Poet and *Center for Fiction* Fellow

"*Fame Shark* chronicles the hip and hilarious adventures of a neurotic, broke New York bookworm named Hazak who's trying to escape his name, his history, his shrink parents and his Jewish guilt. Not easy when he's surrounded by his father's penis paintings, rich and famous friends and the ambitious heartbreaking city itself."
—Susan Shapiro, author of *Speed Shrinking*
and *Five Men Who Broke My Heart*

"An extremely talented new voice, Royal Young in *Fame Shark* novelistically paints a beautiful, funny, raw, heartfelt memoir motivated by the universal desire for attention, against the backdrop of the hip grit of the Lower East Side."
—Alice Feiring, author of *The Battle for Wine and Love:*
or How I Saved the World from Parkerization

"*Fame Shark* is a fast, funny and sometimes squirmingly uncomfortable read as Royal Young digs around in his youth and offers up the tangled roots that led to his near-desperate thirst for celebrity. Young's unflinching memoir adds much to the dialogue about America's quest for adulation, or at least some shiny, sparkling lights."
—Whit Hill, author of *Not About Madonna: My Little Pre-*
Icon Roommate and Other Memoirs

Fame Shark

Heliotrope Books LLC
c/o SB Design
125 East 4th Street
New York, NY 10003

Designed and typeset by Naomi Rosenblatt with Royal Young

Illustrations by Lee Brozgol

Photographs by Amanda Segur

Fame Shark

*Tales of a
Lower East Side Hustler*

Royal Young

 Heliotrope Books

New York

For Mom, Dad, Fury, & E.D., as promised

Author's Note

Names, dates, events, and identifying characteristics of certain people portrayed in this book have been changed for literary cohesion, to protect privacy, so they and I don't get sued, stalked, or splattered across Page Six.

" ... But since he had heard the call of fame,
he could never be still anymore."
— Theodore Dreiser

Part I

1
Touched By Fame

I grew up watching my father make plates that featured penises as centerpieces. Pink, proud, and stiff, encircled by cerulean Greek key, Dad's creations made me feel scared and small. I saw a private part of the man I could not measure up to. At six years old, I lived in a world shaded by his ceramic glazes. There was love and color, but anger, too, in the way he kneaded his clay, palms pounding the rich, wet earth into shapes of his choosing.

He also constructed skull-shaped masks of Republicans and American conservatives from Nancy Reagan to Arnold Schwarzenegger, and was thrilled when they caused a stir in George Bush Sr.'s Washington, D.C. "I chose a skeletal mask because I wish they were dead. I see them as dead," Dad quoted himself from a review in the *New York Guardian* over family dinner. "Now every newspaper in town wants to interview me," he laughed.

My father saw America as tortured and colorful, his early canvases capturing decadently dark theaters drawn from the lost grandeur of the Chicago movie houses of his childhood. Often the seats in my father's imaginary scenes were crowded with clever caricatures of people he knew, family members and friends. They made me think of life as a stage on which figures moved briefly but stunningly until taking their final bows, never knowing that they were being immortalized along the way.

We lived in one of the first artists' co-ops on Eldridge Street, our rat-infested backyard overgrown with ivy. They called me Hazak.

I loved being the son of an emerging celebrity. Dad's usually angry shoulders eased with confidence in the wake of his renown. I wistfully imagined that Dad would take me away, far from the seedy Lower East Side and its crumbling tenements with dark airshafts, crooked streets filled with dangerous wonders, its pickles in vats, and Hasidim rushing to Ratner's while stepping over heroin addicts collapsed in puddles of their own piss.

My dreams came true when my mother and my two-year-old brother, Yuvi, and I took the Amtrak train to D.C., for Dad's big show. (My father was phobic about flying.) In Washington I guzzled Dr. Pepper, giggling and jumping up and down on my impossibly soft Windsor Hotel bed. I couldn't sleep. The night before the opening felt magic. I listened to hushed footfalls on plush hotel corridor carpets, so different from the sirens and cars blasting heavy bass beats into the wild New York nights.

But the next day, at the opening, Dad whined, "Where are all the reporters?" and, "This show is horribly curated." A lone photographer snapped pictures of a large white-walled gallery covered with Dad's death heads and their brightly leering grins. My father looked distinguished with his graying beard and tall, thin frame tucked into a multicolored blazer with pink bowtie. Mom's hazel eyes and short, dark wavy hair shone on Dad's shoulder, where she rested her head. But who was there to appreciate any of it? A crush of people came, clasping my father's hands with smiles and laughter, but soon left, taking their loud cheer with them. They did not stay to see disappointment cloud Dad's face as he pined for something greater, to be forever in the center of that ecstatic attention.

I wondered why his work wasn't hanging in the spacious galleries in SoHo, a few blocks from where we lived in New York. When he took Yuvi and me gallery hopping there, he complained the art was "pretentious" and the busy people selling paintings ignored us.

Also, if Dad had his own shows in Washington, D.C., where the president lived, I didn't understand why we never had money. Dad blamed it on George H. W. Bush and the stifling Republican agenda of prioritizing business at the expense of the arts. I won't exonerate Bush and his ilk, but I would come to find the art world just as much of a country club.

Eventually my father became a low-paid social worker. When I was around six he took a weekend job that didn't interfere with his leftist politics and appealed to his fascination with the darker parts of the human brain; textbooks on depression, sexuality, addiction, and serial killers piled up beside his bedside. Before I could read, I would flip to the glossy inserts in Dad's true crime books, staring at the photos of blood-drenched victims and then at their killers, glaring back at me in infamy.

My father's lost fame haunted me. In first grade in 1991, I drew a convertible car with a smiley face and made my teacher spell the caption: "My dad was on the radio today. Now he is famous."

But the reporters had stopped calling. And my father became increasingly interested in practicing social work skills on my brother and me, and in saving money. That year, 90 percent of all my birthday and Hanukah money started going into a college fund. My parents thought this was smart savings. They had decided to redeem me from juvenile instant gratification. They were stealing my birthday money so I couldn't buy more *X-men* action figures or save up for a television.

"TV makes you stupid," my neuropsychologist mom explained when Yuvi begged her to let us have one. While studying for her PhD and learning Spanish, she supported us by working in the rehab department at St. Vincent's Hospital. Her patients tended to be victims of severe head traumas, motorcycle accidents and construction site tragedies. It seemed my mother had mystical healing powers that she practiced on other people. While she was caring and kind with me, I was fiercely jealous of the restorative love she gave to rehabilitate her patients. It was a selfish, lonely child's fury.

Dad worked weekends at Foundation House, a residence on Houston and Allen Street for recovering junkies with HIV. But he spent weekdays painting and parenting. My parents deemed it optimal for our psychological development to spend time with Dad in his studio, making papier-mâché puppets from *The Wizard of Oz*. I loved this time, surrounded by the colors of his paints and the dark, dusty smell of wet clay. Dad's love and his artist's madness filled the room, inspiring my small hands to grab paintbrushes and adorn my puppet face of The Lion. Yet Dad's wild moods also ran through mine, reflecting and feeding my rages. When our mutt, Blanche, ate the heads off my puppets, Dad screamed and hit her, his eyes wild as an animal's. Blanche's helplessness wrecked me, but I stayed out of Dad's way, cowardly as the Lion trembling in his celluloid jungle.

Yet, I craved revenge on my father's aggression. Not bold enough to face him with my fists, I schemed. Money—particularly the lack of it—was always on Dad's mind. So when he wasn't looking, I started grabbing handfuls of quarters from his change cup, tossed them out the back window of our second-story apartment into the garden, then asked if I could go outside and play. Once there, I would collect the coins.

"Look what I found on the floor!" I proudly showed Mom my loot when she came home from the hospital the first time I plundered my father's treasure.

"That's nice," she said with a distracted nod.

But then one sweltering day my mother was forced to notice my stealing. Hydrants blasted jets of water into the street, and Mom bought me crushed ice covered in coconut syrup from a grinning Dominican man with a pushcart.

"Can I have a soda too?" I asked as we passed the corner bodega.

"There's a limit," she snapped.

"Fine. I have my own money," I replied coolly, unzipping my neon blue fanny pack to reveal a cache of stolen change I'd been saving for weeks.

"Where did you get that?" Mom asked suspiciously.

"I took it," I confessed.

I really wanted attention and absolution, not cash. But instead of being slapped or getting time-out, I endured long, horrible family discussions. I sat between my parents on our orange living-room couch, surrounded by naive paintings of houses on fire and naked women bathing in a lake; a mirror embossed with thin pink flamingoes; and antique furniture rescued from dumpsters.

"Why did you do it?" my father asked, concerned.

"I have needs that aren't being met," I replied, sniffling. By six, I was able to mimic their psychospeak.

"Sweetie, if you want money, all you have to do is ask," Mom explained, gently running her fingers through my hair.

"Really?"

"Of course. We love you," Dad assured me.

"Okay." I hopped off the couch, and consequence-free, went to my room to draw elaborate underground tunnels with my Crayolas while fantasizing about escape.

They lied; my birthday and Hanukah money still kept disappearing into the mysterious Citibank. Whenever I asked for action figures, Twizzlers, or new clothes from the Gap—and not Salvation Army racks—the answer was always "there's a limit."

My drive for more—and all that "more" meant—were not unlike those of my maternal grandmother, fighting to escape her Lower East Side. My Babbi was born in 1932 and raised on Pitt Street and Houston, a few blocks from where I was now growing up. She was the daughter of Orthodox Austrian immigrants who came through Ellis Island in 1919 with thousands of other displaced Jews, gazing in awe at the Statue of Liberty from the steerage deck of a third-class freighter. Marked with chalk as they passed through Ellis Island, labeled like imported produce, they hoped that in this strange new country their children could escape the poverty, persecution, and death of the Old World; that they could learn trades, and shape American educations into money, security, and safety.

The Lower East Side of the '30s was an Eastern European *shtetl* transplant, an unruly Jewish village struggling through the end of the Depression. Its tenements teemed with immigrants who practiced wild customs—matchmaking, interpreting prophesies from dreams—that they'd imported with silver menorahs hidden under rags during the ocean passage. Beneath elevated trains hurtling over Allen Street, downtown Manhattan was filled with poverty, with windowless sweat-shops where thousands of laborers worked fourteen-hour days, where prostitutes leaned against the trembling subway trestles, and Klezmer music whined faintly through the streets.

Babbi got out of there—first by working as a lookout for gamblers as a child, and then as a governess in her teens. Eventually she married, and earned her doctorate degree in child psychology as a young woman. My family had a history of fixing other people's problems and hiding our own.

Babbi couldn't understand why my parents would raise her grand-children in the ghetto she had escaped. But the Lower East Side, the neighborhood their ancestors had already abandoned, was all the new-lyweds could afford, and was the first sacrifice they made for their children. A year before I was born, in 1985, my parents bought our old tenement with other artist bohemians, cleaning out the debris from its former incarnation as a shooting gallery. When they purchased it from the city for $25,000, the building was infested with rodents and crammed with garbage, hypodermic needles, and busted condoms.

"But this is my big money maker! The smartest move I ever made," Dad insisted when his mother-in-law, my Babbi, questioned his decision to live in the dodgy neighborhood. With a team of other eccentrics, he and Mom renovated the building themselves, knocking down walls and plastering sheetrock, while she was pregnant with me.

Six years later, Dad's investment still hadn't paid off. He picked up garbage, weaving it into his artwork or making Yuvi and me wear it. When he saw a down winter coat sprawled on the street between mold-ing fruit and a puddle of fluorescent green radiator coolant, he brought it home and washed it.

"It's a perfectly good *shmata*," he argued, when I refused to touch the stained item.

I would have demanded that he don the filthy finds he brought home, except he always did, proudly displaying his "deals."

Also availing herself of local color, my Jewish mamacita practiced Spanish at Castillo de Jaguar, a bustling restaurant where my Sunday morning breakfasts were eggs over easy, bacon, and home fries—colored orange from sofrito. The waitresses smiled, pinched Yuvi's cheeks, and called him "Papi." With his black hair, dark eyes, and full, pouting lips, he fit in more than grey-eyed, pale-skinned me.

Instead of having playdates, I spent my free time making Mom administer psych tests to me. My ambitious mother's degree now hung in a small, private office near Washington Square Park, where she tested children for dyslexia and attention deficit disorder. My ambition was to have a big problem, like the children who stole her time as she tested them. I imagined my mother's love lay hidden in the runny, black ink blobs of the Rorschach test.

"What do you see in this ink splotch?" she asked with the earnest curiosity of a specialist.

"Superman. Do I have dyslexia?" I replied.

"No." Mom smiled every time she had to dismiss one of my hopeful self-diagnoses. But I figured if I had attention deficit disorder or autism, she wouldn't have to find patients because she could stay home to treat me.

But that never happened. Instead, Dad's studio on the first floor of our building became the site of my messy longings let loose on canvasses, or in stories about suicidal whales that I dictated to him before I could write. Encouraging my taste for tragedy, Dad started reading me bloody bedtime stories. Every night, tucked into the warm crook of his arms, his rough beard brushing the top of my head, we were locked together in beautiful, frightening fantasies.

"Several young men, also flushed with drink, seized anything they could come across—whips, sticks, poles, and ran to the dying mare. Mikolka stood on one side and began dealing random blows with the crowbar. The mare stretched out her head, drew a long breath and died," my father read.

The horse hadn't harmed anyone. I got up and left the room without a word. When I came back, Dad was holding the book open to the same page, glaring at me.

"What is wrong with you? Don't ever walk out of a room while I'm in the middle of a sentence," he shouted.

"It's not fair," I said, crawling under my covers.

"It's Dostoyevsky!" Dad screamed, getting up and taking the book with him. He shut off my light and slammed the door.

At school, the most aggressive girl in my first-grade class was named Patrice. She pinched and hit all the other kids except me. She was a six-year-old bully with cornrows and a smoky voice. One day she whispered, "Let's go to the bathroom to play mommy and daddy."

"I don't want to," I said, pushing her away.

"What's going on here?" our teacher asked, coming over to us.

Though I had engaged in this game with other girls in my class, there was something different about Patrice's aggression; her strong hand was now squeezing my wrist hard. Ashamed and scared, I stared at the floor and just shook my head, blushing.

"Everyone has to have a potty partner," our teacher said, annoyed, scooting us out of the classroom. Patrice led me to the unisex bathroom in the empty faculty lounge, which locked from the inside.

"Show me your dick," Patrice demanded, bolting the door. I shook my head no. Then I looked out the narrow window at blue patches of sky as Patrice pulled down my pants and underwear, touching me and drawing my hand past the straps of her pink overalls. I felt violated, but also strangely wanted and excited, the blood pumping harder to my heart. It was my first taste of being singled out, chosen, carried along on the seductive currents of my own specialness.

When we got out of the bathroom, Patrice's sister, who was in third grade, was waiting. She laughed and shoved us, screaming, "Oooh, you guys were fucking."

My parents, so good at solving their young clients' problems, didn't know I was afraid to go to school. I finally had a real problem, but I was terrified to tell anyone. My name, Hazak, means "strong" in Hebrew, but I felt powerless to stop what was happening to me. My fear and fascination kept me quiet. But I started wearing a cape to school every day. If I pretended I was a superhero, I would have the strength to stop

Patrice's tough, teasing brown fingers.

"Why do you insist on wearing a costume all the time, sweetie?" Mom questioned.

"To save people from bad guys," I said.

"How brave," she smiled, not realizing I was the one desperate for a savior.

My first-grade playground was a hotbed of AIDS urban legends. I thought they would scare Patrice off.

"You're going to die. I heard a man puts HIV needles in pay phone coin holes," I told Patrice.

"No way. He puts them on movie theater seats with the spike up, so it stick you when you sit," she scoffed.

Because of Patrice, I felt like there was a dirty, secret part of me. On our way to visit Babbi and Zayde in Long Island, a homeless man kissed the back of my neck in Penn Station. I felt cold, cracked lips on my skin and turned to see his ragged figure running away through the crowds. Strangers were even more dangerous than my classmate. When Dad and I ran into one of his old friends who asked my name I replied, "Blue fish wrapped in paper." I was afraid to tell him my real one.

By 1993, when I was eight, Patrice was no longer my classmate. But I was left with morbid fantasies about being kidnapped. In taxi cabs I memorized the license plate numbers, just in case I had to yell them out the window to my unsuspecting mother as the murderous cabbie sped away with me still inside.

That winter, my father introduced me to an old friend he called "Fancy Nancy." She lived on the Upper West Side and wanted to take Yuvi and me shopping for the holiday season.

"Don't let Fancy Nancy spoil you," Dad warned. "She's not good with limits like us and will probably buy whatever you want."

"OK," I promised, listening hungrily on the extension as Fancy

Nancy made plans with my mother.

"I'll pick them up after school tomorrow for Christmas shopping," Nancy said.

"Hanukah shopping," Mom corrected. "I'll make latkes for dinner and we'll light the candles when you get back."

As we tried to get a cab the next day on First Avenue and Third Street, an off-duty limousine pulled up. A tinted window rolled down.

"Where ya goin'?" croaked the chauffeur.

"The biggest comic book store nearby," Nancy said.

"Get in," the driver said and jabbed his thumb toward the back.

"Cool car," Yuvi remarked, grinning.

"Come on, this is much more fun than a taxi," Nancy said and beckoned to me.

"I won't," I said. I knew my father would be furious. Liberals did not ride in limousines. I was suddenly certain this luxury trip I wanted so badly would end in a sinister sentence: my abduction and death.

"Sorry, he won't get in," Nancy shrugged.

The limousine took off, the driver scowling and the car's exhaust hanging in the cold air, its acrid fumes the only reminder of my fear.

Later that night, I made Mom tell my favorite family fable. "When you were an infant, I was wheeling you through SoHo and a baby photographer stopped me. She said you were a beautiful baby and could she photograph you? We took you to her studio, but the flashbulbs hurt your light eyes and you wouldn't stop crying no matter what we did. All the photos were ruined."

The next day, I stole one of my father's Sharpies and blacked out Patrice's face in my class picture. I became obsessed with reclaiming my next close-up. If I was famous, my parents would pay closer attention and no one could ever touch me again.

2
Heil Hollywood!

The September after I turned ten, I started The Neighborhood School for fifth grade. I felt adventurous, leaving behind Patrice and my old, dilapidated school building near the fast frenzy of the FDR Drive, surrounded by towers of public housing. My life so far was woven inextricably with the paint-stained, overly sensitive world of my parent's constant and anxious analysis. For all my bursts of hope inspired by new scenery, there was a bruising boredom after the initial excitement, a sadness that surrounded me. I mistook my melancholy for specialness. I knew I was different from my peers and decided it was daring destiny rather than ordinary depression that hovered constantly over my head like a drab halo.

If I couldn't always relate to my friends, if my parents' love sometimes seemed conditional and twisted, then celebrity, where the whole great, grasping, unknowably vast world craved a piece of me, seemed like perfect compensation. At The Neighborhood School teachers were creative, enthusiastic, young and pretty, many jangling bracelets hanging from their thin wrists as they wrote lovely cursive over blackboards, breasts slightly swaying. I was encouraged to be me, or at least a version of myself. A better version, I decided. Even a star.

"Can I be in movies?" I asked Heather, a loud half-Hawaiian, half-Danish girl, one of my new classmates. Her redheaded mom was a casting director who found films that needed large casts of child actors as extras.

"What's your name?" she shot back.

"Hazak Brozgold," I said.

"If you want to be a star you have to have a better name, like Jonathan Taylor Thomas," she scoffed. JTT, as all the girls in my class called him, was the spunky, blonde, Aryan preteen heartthrob of the year. His smile made me furious and filled me with self-hatred: each of his glowing white teeth stood for one of my failures.

But I was as determined as my immigrant ancestors to succeed, and even relished my role as the plump underdog. So when the Metropolitan Opera Guild did an in-school residency program, I quickly landed a role as a friendless bookworm in our elementary opera, *The Bubblegum Tricks of PS 36*. At least I got to open the show with a solo song. I scanned the crowd opening night till I found Heather's mom. Then I performed all my lines as if communing directly with her soul.

"Heather never told me your son loves acting so much. It would be a great experience for him to do some movies," Heather's mom told my mom afterwards.

"As long as it doesn't interfere with Hebrew school and homework," Mom said.

It didn't. When it came to being a child extra in films, Heather's mom took me and every other willing kid in the whole school on as clients, submitting our names and vitals to casting companies. I had no auditions and no lines. I couldn't believe how easy it was and didn't realize this meant anonymous walk-on roles.

"Come in," Dad called when I knocked on his studio door to tell him my amazing news.

"I'm going to be a movie star," I told Dad proudly as he carefully painted the pink nipples and blushing breasts of a nude woman emerging from a seashell like Botticelli's *Birth of Venus*. He often listened to old musicals while working, the same plays that had been performed on the Chicago stages of his youth. Today it was *Gypsy*, one of his favorites that I understood was about a mean mother who was jealous of her daughter's success.

"When I moved from Chicago to New York in the '60s, I wanted to do everything: be a filmmaker and an artist," Dad said.

"Heather's mom says I have great stage presence," I gushed.

"Your Grandpa Morris, my own father, didn't support me emotionally or with money. He still thinks art is a waste of time. You're lucky you have a father like me who knows how important creativity is."

"Why is Grandpa Morris like that?" I asked. At ten, I found Dad's rage toward his own father fascinating. I loved Dad and wanted to hate Grandpa Morris too, for hurting him.

"His second wife, Belle, made him even more selfish than he already was. That was their arrangement," Dad explained.

"What about your mom?" I asked, hoping some of his answers could explain away my own dark thoughts, when I lay in bed worrying that I'd turn into an endless nothing after I died.

"Grandma Evelyn could barely help herself. She was a manic depressive, agoraphobic," Dad analyzed. "She was always vain, imagining herself as an exotic Jewish beauty trapped as a suburban housewife. She would have been thrilled to learn of your acting. I have to go check the kiln."

It seemed Dad loved me only when I was dedicated to his dreams. With the news of my own small triumph, he locked me out of his studio, the space where we had shared so many creative secrets. As he closed his door, I saw his brown eyes grow darker with some pain I couldn't decipher. I went back upstairs to write poems about sad, beautiful women. I was glad Grandma Evelyn would have been proud of me, but I wasn't sure my father, the person who mattered most, was. I feared Grandpa Morris had hurt Dad too deeply, rejecting his art and the life he had made for himself in New York and raising my father to speak only in the language of abandonment, disappointment, loss.

I got the chance to investigate my father and grandfather's relationship more when my Grandpa Morris Brozgold came to visit us.

"Do you believe what Morris said when I offered that he could sleep in our room? Dad asked. "He said, 'I would have nightmares with all those masks.'" Dad fumed.

"Are we allowed to visit him uptown?" I asked.

"Sure, but it won't be fun," Dad warned.

I was excited my grandfather would be staying in a suite at the Hilton Hotel on 54th Street and Avenue of the Americas, thrilled I had fancy family members who could afford the luxury lifestyle I craved.

"When are you going to stop shopping in the trash, son?" My grandfather laughed, nudging Dad after they hugged. Morris was a tall, gaunt man with a flat voice and pale eyes, which we shared. Our similarities both shocked and comforted me, providing a small tear in the too-tight twining between my father and me.

"Thanks for undermining me in front of my kids," Dad growled.

"They're my grandkids and I get to take them shopping," Morris said. "You probably never do."

He took Yuvi and me, his estranged grandchildren, to the FAO Schwarz toy store. In his gray eyes, I looked for the reason why he'd hurt my dad, but couldn't see past the bills he peeled off from wads of money he carried in a gold clip. I remembered Dad telling me he had married into Belle's family, the Feuers, for their money. They owned an insurance agency in Springfield, Illinois, all four Feuer sisters and three Feuer brothers living in the same big house, spotlessly clean. I decided this immaculate life and the thick green stack of currency he held was what my grandfather had traded in his son and grandchildren for.

"Don't spoil them, Dad," my father scolded.

"Oh kid, you'll get your share when I die." Morris smiled as we greedily grabbed action figures.

At the hotel, Yuvi and I gorged on croissants at private continental breakfasts and chugged the small plastic containers of cream meant for coffee, acting like addicts. Feeling like an emperor in Morris's airy suite high above the city I perceived the concrete canyon below as remote and majestic, not untamed and beyond my control. From here the horses and carriages wheeling around Central Park, the crushing tourists taking pictures of what seemed unspectacular sights to me, were far away, easily eradicated if I squinted one eye and lifted two fingers to pinch them into imaginary oblivion. Spreading our packages on the bed while Morris shaved for dinner, Yuvi and I raided his minifridge. I guzzled Coke as we flipped through channels on the large-screen TV. *Man of the House*, starring Chevy Chase and Jonathan Taylor Thomas, was playing. I hated JTT for having the perfect stage name, for shining in such unselfconscious, blonde, all-American wonder.

"Can you change it?" I asked Yuvi, who always insisted on controlling the remote.

"Leave it. I like this kid," Dad said, laughing.

I wanted him to chuckle at my jokes. Despite Dad's disdain for television in his own home, when a set was turned on anywhere else, he watched it with greedy scrutiny, eyesight tunneled on the flatly moving figures. The child actor's golden bowl cut infuriated me. My hair was a wavy Hebrew mane and wouldn't stay in that kind of hairstyle.

"What is this *goyische drek*?" Grandpa Morris asked, pouring himself a Diet Coke and water, because of his diabetes.

"When I'm in movies they'll be way better, duh," I said.

"This kid is going to be the first star in our family. I can feel it." Grandpa Morris ruffled my hair.

"He's only going to be an extra, Dad." My father rolled his eyes.

My first movie was *Bed of Roses*, a romantic comedy with Christian Slater and Mary Stuart Masterson. The set was in an old school with big oak banisters. There was a giant black camera on a mechanical track. I was assigned an actress to play my mom for a crowd scene where we had to move our lips, but not speak. She had honey hair feathered out from her face and frank blue eyes.

"Why don't we play a game to pass time. It's forever between takes," she suggested.

"My dad and I play this game called Geography where I name a place and you have to say a place that starts with the same letter mine ends in." I had mastered this and wanted to impress her.

"You start," she smiled.

"Yucatan," I said, showing off.

"New Mexico," she returned.

I was ecstatic. I imagined she was my real mother. How cool would it be to have a mom who was a rising movie star, could help me learn the ropes, and catapult me to acclaim? Then I felt guilty for wanting to leave Mom behind. I saw her warm, dark shape rushing into my room as I rose from another bloody nightmare, the streets of the Lower East Side still filled with the shadows of vampires in my mind. Her hands with their long, shaped nails gently scratching my scalp as she rhythmically combed the stubborn hair from my teary eyes.

"This is my mom," I said as I introduced my fake to my real mother when she came to pick me up later.

"He's so smart! He beat me in Geography." My screen mom shook my real mom's hand.

"Oh, we play that game a lot. Venezuela?" my mother laughed, testing me.

"Atlantic City!" I answered her.

When *Bed of Roses* came out, my whole class went to a private premiere at Loews Cineplex on 34th Street. Mom and Yuvi came with me.

"You're famous now, like dad," he said.

"I wish he was here," I told him.

"Your father's studio time is very precious," Mom said, smoothing my hair. "He can see it when it comes out on video."

I shoved free buttered popcorn into my mouth as the lights dimmed. I told myself I was glad Dad wasn't there. He never bought me snacks at the movies, insisting we smuggle in cheaper soda and burnt, homemade popcorn from outside, the black plastic bags rustling as we took our seats.

The film started with Mary Stuart Masterson, the sympathetic heroine, crying over her dead father and her lifeless goldfish. Christian Slater, the creepily romantic male lead, falls in love with her shadow and sends her flowers as a mystery admirer. Not fully relating to the adult passions, I kept getting distracted looking for myself in the background. I recognized my city, the Ottendorfer Library on Second Avenue where Dad took me after school, the twin towers shining in the skyline, and finally, there I was, with the yellow sweater and neon-striped book bag leaving a school building.

"Look, Hazak, it's you," Mom laughed, pointing.

I smiled as I walked off screen. The movie kept going, and my eyes lingered longingly on the last shot of Christian Slater's lush roof garden. Like in Morris's hotel room, the peaks and towers of the city held power for me. It seemed that if I had my own fantasy forest in the middle of New York, perched between the rusting water towers and faded stone faces of the tenement turrets, I might find a peace to fill me. On the city's sidewalks, I was always craning my neck to look up at the impossible height of skyscrapers, longing to be at the top. Being part of a movie, something so many people would witness, made me feel bigger than buildings, and real. As the credits rolled and the theater lights came up, all I could think about was when I could be on screen again. The theater, emptying of viewers made life seem emptier than before. Back at home, I begged my parents to get me more extra roles. If I could be on movie screens, they would have to see me.

"That world just sets you up for disappointment," Dad warned.

"I'm already disappointed," I insisted.

"Fine," he said, stalking out of our apartment and stomping loudly downstairs to his studio. Mom stayed on the couch.

"I want to be in movies too," six-year-old Yuvi announced from the floor where he had been playing with our white mutt Blanche and listening.

"Please?" I begged.

"I'll talk to Heather's mom," Mom promised.

The next day, my name was on the list of kids who would be in *Ransom*, which my teacher passed out after taking attendance. I read that the film was about a young boy being kidnapped, starred Mel Gibson and Rene Russo, and was directed by Ron Howard. I imagined the child actor playing Mel Gibson's son getting sick on set and the crew grabbing me as his stand-in. I was afraid of auditioning for larger roles, but being discovered was different. The majority of all our "extra" paychecks went to the PTA and the rest to my parents, who shuttled it quickly into my college account. Yet surely, with all the cameras that had so suddenly entered my life, one would capture an image of me that was stronger and more vibrant than my image of myself. This boy would be worth something.

"You need to sign this permission slip, so I can be in *Ransom* with

Mel Gibson and Rene Russo," I proudly told my parents as we sat down to family dinner that evening. Every night at six, Mom rang a small bronze gong hanging from the kitchen ceiling, calling us to eat together. She had made my favorite dish, tuna casserole with Lipton's Cream of Mushroom soup and crunchy Lays potato chips on top.

"I bet Mel Gibson is an anti-Semitic asshole," Dad said pouring himself a giant glass of Coca-Cola.

"What's anti-Semitic?" Yuvi asked.

"Someone who hates Jews," Dad replied between mouthfuls. "He seems like that type."

"What would make you think that? I'm sure Mel is very nice," said Mom, her eyes distraught at the thought that Mel Gibson could hate our kind.

"I'm sure he's not! All those big macho movie types are Republican assholes " Dad cried, eagerly underlining that we were still shunned by the powerful in America. For my father any non-Jew who had achieved that level of power or status must be an anti-Semite. Every now and then he was right.

"Who cares about him anyway? I'll be in it," I boasted.

The next morning at 5 a.m., I was picked up with my class by a bus with cushy white leather seats. As we glided uptown, I looked through the tinted windows at businessmen with jobs unlike my father's, wearing green trench coats and balancing briefcases and coffee. The streets above 14th Street were clean and swept, as we swiftly rushed to meet the morning light breaking through the trees of Central Park. We pulled up at the New York Coliseum at Columbus Circle and filed into a huge hall filled with extras. The food table gleamed with glazed donut holes, a sugary oasis of free treats. I suddenly found myself important enough to stuff my face with this smorgasbord, shocked to find myself no longer just a nerdy boy in my messy bedroom on a lost corner of Delancey Street. The world of Hollywood, I felt, was already starting to transform me.

"I love your face, but these clothes need to go," a young woman said as she dragged me into the wardrobe area. "Here. If you wear these you can be a walk-on." She tossed me a pair of navy sailor pants.

"But where can I change?" I looked around in dismay at the packed auditorium, ten times the size of the one at The Neighborhood School. This was even worse than getting naked for Patrice. Anyone could run up and grab me.

"Look, if you want to be in movies, forget modesty," the woman barked, disappearing behind racks of dresses.

I hid in a corner and tried to squeeze into the pants she had handed me. I sucked in my stomach, pulling the thick fabric together till a top button popped off. I was too fat. I crumpled the costume in a corner and rushed to Craft services to consume donut holes, my belly bulging and rumbling with secret shame.

Another bus soon arrived to pick up the extras and took us to Bethesda Fountain in Central Park, where a huge science fair scene was set up. Curious passersby and paparazzi were drawn toward the sprawling set, hoping to catch a glimpse of stars. I had never seen so many people shoving each other and screaming in excitement. I feared I would get lost in the throng and was suddenly suspicious of the strangers who had come for *Ransom*. I imagined I would be kidnapped by women who wanted to tie me up and touch my penis in a dark cellar where rats were eating my fingers. I imagined the *New York Post* headlines: RISING STAR SNATCHED FROM ABDUCTION PRODUCTION.

Between takes, my friend John John, a ten-year-old fellow actor, and I wriggled out from behind our science fair booth and snuck over to where Mel Gibson paced in front of a huge green screen. An assistant was running behind him with hairspray and a comb, trying to hide his bald spot.

"Excuse me, Mr. Gibson, can I please have your autograph?" I asked in awe.

Mel looked down at me in disgust without responding. His eyes flicked back to the assistant.

"I'm going to lunch. I'll be back in four hours," he said. His bloodshot blue eyes swept over me like I didn't exist before he stalked away. I recalled my father's warning and feared Mel had smelled my Hebrew blood. "Nazi," I shouted at Mel's back. But he never turned around. "Don't get us in trouble," John John grabbed my hand and pulled me toward Rene Russo who was surrounded by extras, but making her way through the crowd in slow motion.

"Excuse me, Ms. Russo, may I please have your autograph?" John John asked.

She laughed, pointing to the cameras. "Honey, we're still rolling."

I cringed and tried to hide behind John John as an angry voice shouted "Cut!" But Rene Russo just tossed back her long strawberry-colored hair, knelt, and signed her name for both of us.

"When I'm famous, I'll always sign my name for kids. I promise," I told her.

But the scraps of paper from my school composition book holding star signatures weren't enough for me. I wanted to prove the woman in wardrobe, Mel Gibson, and Dad wrong by landing a starring role. If I could just find the director, Ron Howard, and impress him, he'd cast me. Mom told me he had started acting young. I hoped he would recognize we weren't so different. Someone must have given him a chance, and now I hoped he'd give me one. I ran through the crowd, ducking to avoid a boom pole, leaping over light stands till I spotted the man who had yelled "cut" by himself, watching footage on TV screens. Trying to play it cool, I walked up and asked, "Excuse me, sir, can I have your autograph?"

He beckoned me closer, looking around to make sure no one was watching.

"Look, kid, if I say yes to you, I'm going to have to say yes to everyone and I'm really busy—people will mob me."

I was disappointed, but also amazed that this man's smallest action could trigger a stampede.

"Ok, thanks." I started to walk away.

"Wait. How about a handshake?" he called.

I rushed back and shook his hand; it was even better than a scrawled name. When our fingers met, I willed some of his power to course through me. But I didn't have the courage to ask for my big break. My head was crammed and confusing: my Id was screaming for stardom, my Superego sternly stepping in to shout louder—*You don't deserve it!*

When I got back to The Neighborhood School on Monday, Heather wasn't in class.

"Why isn't Heather in school today? Is she sick?" I asked my teacher.

"No, her mom moved her to private school at Friends Seminary."

Private school. The words conjured an ivy-walled fortress where kids were taught the secrets to success. It was as if Heather, having reached a certain level of celebrity (she had done a cereal commercial), had naturally moved on the next plane, leaving me behind. As always, there seemed to be something inside me, a rottenness I was born with, leaking some ooze of failure over my life. As always, I channeled my frustrated passion into performance.

That night, I put on an interpretive dance in the living room with Mom and Dad as captive audience. I used my humidifier as a smoke machine and screwed blue-colored lightbulbs into the lamps. I draped sheets over the furniture, the ghostly shapes framing my gyrating to Mom's Israeli folk albums playing on the stereo.

"Great job!" Dad clapped when I was done. "You're really serious about this performing thing."

"How would you like to go to acting classes so you can dance and act there?" Mom asked.

"I like working with real movie stars," I said.

"They don't care about you and that's not a choice," Dad laughed.

"I know you think being ten isn't a big deal, but this is my life," I shouted at him.

"Sure, Hazak, you'd be great on a soap opera." Dad kept chuckling.

Two days later, Dad picked me up from school and started leading me toward the F train's Second Avenue stop.

"Where are we going?" I asked him.

"Acting class at Tada!" Dad smiled. Tada! was a well-known youth theater program in the city.

"I told you I don't want to go. I won't," I said. I stopped, grabbing the rail on the subway steps.

"Oh yes you are, Mister. I'm not sitting through more of your performances. I'm getting you the professional help you need." Dad pried at my fingers, then shoved me under the turnstile so he didn't have to pay my fare.

When we got off the train at 23rd and Sixth Avenue, I realized the neighborhood wanted to be everything at once, like me. Big African men sold incense and bootleg Gucci bags. Clueless commuters and tourists ventured out of Penn Station on 34th. The XXX shops had naked people with red stars covering their privates in their windows. And Hasidim shouted about discounts from storefronts full of camcorders and big TV screens that played my image as I passed by.

In acting class at Tada! we had to introduce ourselves by improvisation exercises where we stated our first name then had to come up with an adjective that described us and also started with the first letter of our name.

"My name is Hazak. I'm Hopeful."

Then I warmed up with the musical scales while my overenthusiastic drama teacher, a tubby middle-aged man with a mushroom cut, yelled, "Diaphragm! Project from your diaphragm! Sing! Sing! Sing!" as he smacked his palm on an old piano in need of tuning.

At the end of my first month-long class we put on a small show for our parents, which consisted of patched together improvs and a big finale song. I couldn't help but lick my lips nervously when I was on stage. Having to remember lines was way harder than being scene filler in films. Finally, my whole ensemble marched onto the barren stage in pancake makeup and red Tada! T-shirts. I shoved my way to center as I bellowed: *"Tada! Here we are, the biggest thing in little kids."*

As we sang, I picked out Mom and Dad in the darkened audience, smiling as they watched me. Then I noticed a homeless man sneak through the curtained entrance and slip up behind Mom. I wanted to scream and point to him, but too fast, he grabbed her purse and dashed out. My mother jumped up, running after him. Dad sat there, unaware of the theft in the dim theater. Even though I was petrified that Mom would be murdered I kept on smiling, grimly repeating in my head the line Dad had told me from *Gypsy*: the show must go on. I danced until the red velvet curtains dropped on polite applause.

"I'm sorry, sweetie," Mom said, hugging me as I rushed up to her. "I missed the rest. I had to cancel all my credit cards and call the police."

"Are you okay?" I searched with my hands for blood or gaping wounds.

"I'm fine and you're a great actor," she said as she smoothed my hair.

"I don't know. Your tongue kept darting out and licking your lips like a lizard. Looked like a nervous newt to me," Dad said.

I decided I wanted to leave Tada! for good and go back to doing extra work in films. I would have rather gorged on donuts, autographs, and bonding sessions with Ron Howard. Seeing Mom getting robbed in a seedy setting was scary. I knew my parents couldn't afford to send me to classes where their wallets would be stolen.

"Fine, you want it so bad, you got it," Dad told me. "But this is your last chance."

One of my father's friends got me a screen test for Nickelodeon. When I was alone in front of the camera with my script, standing before some strange grown-ups who had flown in from Los Angeles as judges, I suddenly stuttered. Dad watched in a corner with his arms crossed. As I tried to read from the pages that were going wobbly in front of my eyes, someone called out, "Nice try kid. Maybe next time."

Dad whistled "Everything's Coming up Roses" as we left, with a smug "I told you so" look on his face. I was crushed by his pleasure over my failure more than by not being able to pass my only audition. Walking home through dirty city streets, I wondered why Dad didn't want me to be famous. He always talked about how furious he was Grandpa Morris never supported his art. The only reason I could think of was that he was jealous.

"Hey, why don't we make some drawings when we get home?" Dad asked.

"Sounds great," I grinned up at him. But I was acting.

3
Family Fame Fables (Fuck)

My maternal grandparents Babbi and Zayde supported everything that had to do with the arts. Their three-story house in Great Neck, Long Island, was crammed with Zayde's impressionist paintings and Babbi's sculptures. They even bought Dad's artwork and hung a papier-mâché mask on their walls: a thick-lipped frowning man's face with a flaming pink and yellow Toucan emerging from the top of his head. They put on plays every Purim. In the sunroom addition to their Great Neck home, Zayde hammed it up as homicidal Haman and Babbi played the regal and resourceful Esther, beautiful queen who delivered the Jews. They drove into the city after my eleventh birthday on June 17th, to cultivate my artistic palate, and took Yuvi and me to the Museum of Natural History and to *Tosca* at the Metropolitan Opera, where a random woman spilled scalding coffee on my arm during intermission. She noticed, but walked away without a word of apology.

"Did you guys have fun today?" Mom asked, when we picked up her and Dad on Eldridge Street in Babbi and Zayde's car later that evening.

"We saw a big blue whale hanging from the ceiling," Yuvi said.

"And some bitch spilled coffee on my arm at the opera," I added.

"Now, Hazak, express how you really feel instead of using a curse. It doesn't mean anything," Mom chided.

"'Bitch' is exactly how I feel," I said.

"What do you think of the old neighborhood?" Dad asked Babbi.

"*Zaest Frim an alta shtudt macht a naya shtudt*—from an old city, we make a new one. I used to be the toughest girl boxer on Houston Street," Babbi said. She brushed back her dyed blonde hair in the overhead mirror and shakily applied bright orange lipstick that smeared around the edges of her full mouth. "But when your Zayde taught me art at the Educational Alliance, I knew I was going to marry him. His people were depressed Litvak Jews, but the Kuglers were strong-willed Galicians. We came from Austria, where my father graduated from a gymnasium. He always told us we could go as far as we wanted. Never take less. Always more."

"My father never went to school or even spoke a single word to me," Zayde admitted.

"Oh, Chaim, your father was a difficult man," Babbi patted his knee.

"Stop the car, that was Yolanda," Dad shouted from the backseat where we were squished.

"Do something," Mom gasped.

Yolanda was a prostitute who'd befriended my parents while she walked the streets around our building. Dad leaped out, running to where Yolanda and another woman were scratching at each other's faces, ripping out chunks of weave. Yolanda's legs were too skinny in shiny black tights; the silver studs on her leather jacket flashed as her pocked arms swung viciously through the thick night air. Through the car windows I watched my suddenly superman social worker father separating the women and talking them down. Finally Dad got back in the car. "Yolanda was fucking that lady's husband," he explained.

"Pathetic," Babbi clucked.

"Fuck!" Yuvi shouted.

"That's inappropriate language for a six-year-old," Zayde said as he cleared his throat.

"I can handle this," Dad answered. He glared at his father-in-law.

"Motherfucker," I laughed.

"They're strong-willed, like me. *Gefayrlich*—It's fated." Babbi just shrugged in her pastel jumper.

"Desperate times call for desperate measures," Dad warned me. "I'm going to start charging you a nickel for every swear word you use."

"If I charged you, you'd probably owe me a million fucking dollars," I pointed out.

"Five cents!" Dad shouted. "I'm the father and I make the rules around here."

He got to do all the things I couldn't, like curse all day in his studio and sketch naked people. He spent so much time striving to be a successful artist, why wasn't I allowed to act in movies?

I couldn't watch any of my old favorite films, because seeing Macaulay Culkin in *Home Alone* made me feel too jealous. Instead, I swore like George Carlin, the raspy-voiced comedian I'd seen on Babbi and Zayde's TV. Dad implemented "desperate measures," dragging me to summer day camp where I feared I would sink into the desperate anonymity of the neighborhood kids. I saw them summer after summer, sitting on the same stoops, their voices scratchy and their eyes hard too young. The counselors were not much older than me, sixteen-year-olds hired from the Pitt Street projects surrounding the Henry Street Settlement. They stepped on my Payless shoes and pushed me out of the way in the dark stone halls that wound through the basement of the Settlement.

My talents as an artist saved me. Even the older kids asked me to draw for them, marveling at my creations. It seemed artistic talent could be bartered for safety. The way I splashed bright strokes of paint, the freedom that overtook me while dancing across the empty stages of Settlement playhouses that dated back to my grandmother's time, helped me survive. Fellow campers whose lives at home were crowded into small project rooms and stairways where lights flickered, always broken, recognized in me a means of escape. Wanting to get out was something we all shared.

When Mom picked me up, after summer days at the Settlement, she took Yuvi and me to visit Zayde's mother, our great-grandmother, *alte* Babbi Sarah, in an apartment in the East River Housing projects full of glue mousetraps. Babbi Sarah had been born beautiful in Russia, but now she smelled like stale sour cream and sat in her kitchen all day with a Jamaican nurse Zayde paid for. Though Mom cooked delicious roast chicken for Dad, our house was not *glatt* kosher, it was contaminated by the experimental turkey stroganoff Dad cooked. Mismatched dishes were balanced precariously on top of each other in our house and we ate off them, devouring meat and dairy, unconcerned about the dietary restrictions imposed by Babbi Sarah's version of God. Mom bought big meals at Ratner's for Babbi Sarah, including my favorite, cheese blintzes.

"*Ees eet kosher?*" Babbi Sarah asked.

"*Gloib Mir*—of course." Mom reassured her.

"Your momma vas a beautiful actress, *Bubbeleh*," Babbi Sarah said as she pinched my cheeks.

"No she wasn't! She diagnoses dyslexia," I answered and wriggled away from her wrinkled fingers.

"Actually, I worked in the *Folksbiene* Theater in high school," Mom blushed. "It was a real honor because I was so young. The *Folkspiene* is the oldest Yiddish theater in the country."

"Did you act?" I asked hungrily.

"I was in Peretz Hirshbein's *Grine Felder—Green Fields*," Mom explained. "It was a love story. In one scene, I jumped through a window and shouted '*Ch'bin doo!*'—'I'm here!' I loved it," she giggled.

"What happened?" I asked.

"What do you mean?" She looked far away as she reminisced.

"Why did you stop?"

"Well, it was fun, but it just wasn't practical. I had a great time but I wanted to visit Israel and then I met Yakov," she trailed off.

"So you know how I feel. I miss being in movies so much," I confessed.

"I know you had fun, sweetie." Mom smiled. "But you need to think about what you want to be when you're older. Have some food."

"I'll always want to be famous," I told her.

"I'll always want ice cream," Yuvi demanded.

"Shut up, asshole. I'm serious," I shouted.

"Hazak, this is unacceptable behavior. One more word like that to your brother and we're having a family discussion with Dad when we get home."

"But fame is in my genes! Zayde told me we come from generations of cantors who sang for their suppers plus you were a Jewish star!" I wanted to scream at her.

"Yuvi, we can stop at Baskin Robbins on the way back. My treat,"

Mom offered, turning to spoon blintz into Babbi Sarah's faded face. My great-grandmother, her head wrapped in a babushka, just stared at her as she was fed.

"Sorry," I apologized to my brother as we went into Babbi Sarah's living room to watch *Pinky and the Brain* take over the world on the flickering TV. Still a rare treat, even if the picture was black and white with waves of color sporadically washing over the cartoon antics.

"It's okay," he grinned. "I'm going to get mint chocolate chip with gummy bears."

><

When I was in movement class at Henry Street, I felt like I could conquer the globe. These summer sessions replaced the rush I had gotten at Tada! despite my initial reluctance. My teacher was a lithe, afro-ed woman who blasted Michael Jackson's "Beat It" on a boom box the size of Danny DeVito. I twirled deliriously in a dance studio full of light and lined with mirrors, practicing for a talent show for parents at the end of summer. I could prove to Mom I was serious. I was sure once she saw me on stage she'd remember how exhilarating it was and encourage me to get back into film.

In the meantime, I tried to impress her with learning how to swim and making friends. John John, a kid from my fifth grade, was in my camp group. He was black, had boundless energy and big front teeth that stuck out wide in his splendid smile, and was a constant and en-thusiastic exaggerator. We'd never really talked, outside of getting in trouble with Mel Gibson on the set of *Ransom*, but I invited him to visit Babbi and Zayde's pool in Long Island.

"I know how to swim," he boasted on the Long Island Railroad.

"That's great, John John. Hazak is still learning, maybe you can give him some pointers," Mom suggested.

"I bet you don't really know," I accused.

"I do too," he stuck out his tongue. "I'll show you."

"No kids in the pool until I can supervise," Mom said.

Yuvi and I could barely doggie paddle, and we had been practicing swimming in Babbi and Zayde's pool all summer. Behind their brick house with the green shutters and the vines and flowers crawling around the corners of their stilted porch, my passion for pretending I had a different life was easy to indulge. Mom loved the water, diving and laughing as she swam quickly up the length of the pool to catch us in the shallow end. Our days there were filled up with a kind of buoyancy, and with perhaps what I yearned for more than fame: weightlessness. I wished I could move fast and strong like Mom did in the water, but the deep end scared me: all that space under my feet, and the bottom—a hungry emptiness that hinted at the same in me.

"Do not get in until I come out there," Mom reminded us again as she headed toward Babbi's bathroom to change after we arrived at my grandparents' house.

"Don't worry," I cried and ran out the screen door with John John right behind. I'd decided I wanted to catch John John in what I was sure was a lie.

"Look what I can do," I said, donning a green, donut-shaped inner tube made to look like an alligator. Holding onto the side of the pool, I shimmied around the deep end, pretending I wasn't petrified.

"That's nothing. Watch this," John John said as he moved toward the edge of the pool.

"Maybe you should wait for my mom," I said.

"I told you I know how to swim. Don't be a pussy." John John laughed.

He slipped the alligator around his slim waist and put one foot in the water.

"It's freakin' cold," he yelled.

"You're the pussy. You're not even swimming," I pointed out.

"I just need to get used to it," he answered, giving me the finger and splashing down the pool steps. He held on to the edge of the pool while he shimmied into the deep end.

"You're still not swimming," I called.

"I'll show you," he replied. John John tried to turn toward me and slipped out of the tube. He went under the water, then burst back up thrashing and screaming. His terrible lie was revealed in his terror.

"Hold on! I'll help you," I cried. I ran around the pool shouting for Mom and trying to save John John with the cleaning pole. But he stopped struggling and sank down until all I could see was his dark body underneath eleven feet of water with the sunlight playing across it.

Mom rushed out and paused, eyes darting over the scene before running down the wooden patio steps. She dove head first into the water, and I watched as her pale shape swam to meet his, her fingers scooping him up, the two of them floating to the surface. John John's eyes had rolled back into his head, so I could only see the whites.

"What the fuck did you do?" Mom screamed as she pumped his chest out on the deck and water poured from his mouth. My mom never cursed.

"Nothing. I just wanted to practice for you." I was shaking.

"You let him go in the pool after I told you not to? Oh my god, oh my god." She put her mouth over John John's so it looked like they were kissing.

"Wake up, please," Mom cried.

John John coughed and she locked her lips over his again. I felt nauseous and ran into the house. I hid under my grandparent's grand piano sobbing as ambulance sirens wailed outside. Dad had taught me all about the subconscious and I feared I had secretly wanted John John to drown.

"You can come out now, your mother took John John to the hospital," my grandmother said. Babbi leaned down and smiled at me under the piano.

"I'm never leaving here," I moaned.

"It's not your fault," Babbi told me. "The doctors will pump any water left out of his stomach and lungs and he'll be fine."

She coaxed me into the kitchen with a toasted bagel smothered in butter and blueberry jam.

"My mom thinks it's my fault," I said.

"That boy was a stupid liar for saying he could swim. He could have got himself killed," she said.

"But mom screamed at me like I had murdered him." I wiped my runny nose between bites.

"Your mom is a fragile person. She has been since she was born. She's a passive-aggressive character," Babbi told me.

"What's passive aggressive?" I asked.

"It means she holds things inside her until she expresses her anger at the wrong person," Babbi explained.

"But if she's not mad at me, who is she mad at?"

"Maybe your father," my grandmother said. "I don't know these things. But you're a smart boy with a beautiful heart. Now go watch your X-Men cartoon. You'll feel better. You'll see."

Mom didn't say a word or look at me the whole train ride home. The next day in summer camp, John John avoided me at lunchtime, and over the next week he stopped talking to me altogether. I didn't feel better. I hated John John. He had turned Mom against me. I wouldn't even consider getting in the water. I was too scared I would die. Every Friday as all the other kids excitedly got ready to walk over to the Pitt Street pool, I panicked. I "forgot" my bathing suit so that I would be allowed to sit on the sidelines, safe from the tumult of water games. I was even afraid of trying to float, knowing my limbs had lost all their hollow magic.

A week later, at the summer talent show, in front of a packed house, I sweated through "Thriller," completely obscured by the older dancers who had been placed in front of me. Even though I threw all my energy into the set, no one could see me.

"You were great!" Mom said afterwards. She had tulips for me at the pizza party after the show. My performance had won her forgiveness.

"Like the Yiddish theatre?" I asked.

"Even better," she hugged me.

"You were cool as a cucumber. Why'd they stick you all the way in the back?" asked Dad, taking a photo of me on the empty stage.

"You really liked it?" I asked, blushing.

"Yes, and the bird sculpture you made in art class has pretty good contours." Dad grinned. "I've been working on a commission from the MTA for the Essex Street station. How would you like to pose for one of the murals?"

"Yes, yes, yes!" I shouted, jumping up and down.

"Okay, fold your arms over the book, but look up at me and stay very still," Dad instructed, as I posed in his studio for a sketch the next day. I wanted to prove I was the best model ever. I tried not to move a muscle, not to even blink. I watched my father's face frown in concentration as his pencil scratched at his pad.

"Can I see it when you're done?" I asked after twenty minutes.

"Shhh, no talking," Dad instructed.

I couldn't help watching the hands of the clock tick till I had been stationary for an hour.

"OK, we're finished," he said. He turned the pad to present me with my portrait—pale eyes and an oval face framed by wavy brown hair. I didn't have to be in movies to get famous. Seeing my face immortalized in my father's art was way cooler than fading into the background of film frames. I was finally up front and center in the landscape of the city I lived in and the work of the father I loved.

When the final mural was unveiled, a reception for my dad was held on the Delancey and Essex Street station platform. The F train rumbled through Dad's party as I searched the mural for my image. I pushed through the crowd of MTA officials and curious crackheads to get a closer glance. In the middle of the mural was a bearded man who reached up to the ceiling, looking like Dad would if he was a Greek statue in grey with stern eyebrows and a long, flowing beard. On either side of him were panels with separate frames, each featuring a different Lower East Side incarnation. I recognized Mom wearing a *babushka* and standing over the *Shabbos* candles. Then I saw my frame. There was something wrong with it. The book was open in front of me, I was wearing the same blue sweater, but my skin was brown and I had a tight, curly afro.

"Dad, there's a mistake. You made me black," I said as I ran up to him.

"Calm down. Artistic choice. It looked better that way." Dad shrugged.

I stared at the painting in horror. Not only was I unrecognizable, it seemed my father also wanted to replace me: the two dark eyes of an almost-drowned boy stared back at me.

4
Naked Death

"I don't like traveling because of my bitch mother. She never left the house," my father explained, when I asked if we could take a vacation. "If we go anywhere, we go as a family." His stubborn fear of flying and abandonment kept us stuck in New York.

By sticky August, after John John's almost drowning and Dad making me black for every subway rider on the F train line to see, I wanted to get away from the Lower East Side. My parents didn't believe in air conditioning and I was suffocating at home. I was too traumatized to enjoy Babbi and Zayde's pool and wanted to go where celebrities mingled with civilians so I could be discovered.

"When are we going to Southampton?" I appealed to Mom, interrupting her on the phone with clients. She held up one finger for silence without even looking at me.

"Bitch," I whispered under my breath, copying Dad.

Babbi's rich brother, my great-uncle Larry, had a mansion in Southampton—but we were never invited. He had grown up poor on the Lower East Side with my Babbi. Now he was a millionaire banker. Mom told me he took a helicopter to work every morning and never talked to the rest of the family. I was determined to infiltrate what I imagined was Larry's castle, built on the dunes and facing out to sea. But how to get there? We were stuck in Lower Manhattan with my father.

Vacation for Dad was a walk around the block, something familiar, in an environment he controlled. On breaks from working in his studio he took Yuvi and me to Hamilton Fish Library on Houston Street. It was down the block from the public pool at Pitt Street and the sounds of sprinklers and happily splashing swimmers made me shiver. I wanted to hide in the quiet stacks of books, sitting for hours safe with *Harriet the Spy* and the Stanley children from *The Headless Cupid*. Dad browsed the true crime section; he was addicted to real stories of madness and murder, about monsters like Ted Bundy and a mother who systematically murdered all nine of her children. Yuvi searched the videos for movies he wanted to watch on the TV he didn't have. Afterwards, Dad took us to the Golden Dragon, a Chinese take-out place across the street where we could get four fried chicken wings for $2.00 and Dad would let us order Cokes, our shared sugary addiction.

"When I first got to New York from Chicago in '64, I called them pop," Dad said as we shared our sodas, laughing at this rare good memory from his past.

On one of our trips to the Golden Dragon, Yuvi was chewing ravenously on the tip of his wing when his face suddenly became red and tears streamed down his round cheeks as he gasped for air. I thought he was just joking; he was always acting out to get our parents' attention: breaking eggs on the kitchen floor; stuffing the toilet with newspaper; letting our mother's favorite coffee mugs fall from his pudgy hands and shatter into glass shards around his feet.

"Are you okay?" Dad asked, slapping Yuvi hard on the back.

Yuvi's face was turning purple as he choked.

"Oh my God, oh my God!" my father hollered at no one. "We need a cab to the emergency room right now."

My own throat was starting to close in panic. If our father wanted to pay for a taxi, this must be really serious. Dad grabbed Yuvi by the hand and dragged him out of the take-out place while the workers looked on in horror from behind their bulletproof glass. They shouted at each other in Chinese and starting running away into the kitchen. As we dashed into a taxi I started to hyperventilate.

"St. Vincent's Hospital as fast as you can," Dad yelled at the cabbie. "My son is dying here."

St. Vincent's was where Yuvi and I had been born. Now it was where he would die. I burst into tears.

"Shut up!" Dad's angry voice snapped in my ear.

I tried to stop sobbing as we pulled up to the hospital where Mom now worked. Yuvi was still gasping and crying, his small hands clutching his throat.

"I already have one hysterical kid on my hands," Dad screamed at me. "I don't need two, now get a grip on yourself."

Stunned, I followed him and Yuvi into the ER past shrill ambulances whose red lights blurred my vision.

"A small piece of chicken bone scraped his throat," said a nurse, as she lay my now calm brother down on an examination table.

"Is everything ok?" Mom rushed in, breathless.

"Everything's fine, Doc," the nurse said, reassuring her. "Just a scary accident for a seven-year-old. Looks like a small piece of bone scratched his throat on the way down. He should eat ice cream and chicken soup for a few days."

"Thank God," Mom cried, hugging Yuvi.

"See? Nothing to get upset about," Dad said, turning to me.

You were the one freaking out like a maniac, I wanted to point out, but I was too relieved that Yuvi was safe. I said nothing.

There were block parties around our neighborhood for most of the summer. A Pentecostal church next door to us shut down Eldridge Street every week and blasted music and sermons while they sold *arroz y habichuelas* with hunks of *chicharones* on the side. That summer, Puff Daddy's cover of "Missing You" came out. Dedicated to gunned-down Biggie Smalls, I heard it at least fifteen times a day blasted on big boom boxes tuned to Hot 97. In between songs a minister would get on a plywood podium and shout impassioned speeches in Spanish where the only word I could understand was "Dios."

All day and into the night the parties reigned. I loved this part of the Lower East Side, its streets exploding with energy. As if we, the people of my neighborhood, could harness for just a summer night the reckless, careening current of New York and dance with it, sing loud enough to quiet our collected loneliness. I wished I could run out into the streets, but instead I sat inside, my legs cramped underneath me, my whole, growing body stuffed into our front windowsill, as I stared out until Mom told me to go to bed. This was urban worship, and way more exciting than being dragged to hushed synagogues where my grandfather, Zayde, gave long, boring monologues in Hebrew from the stage, their *bimah*. I had to stand still so long my feet hurt. Even though Dad had been brought up Jewish, he hated going to *shul*, proclaiming he was atheist until he discovered Buddhism. I resented having to go to Hebrew school every Sunday to train for my Bar Mitzvah—and said so.

"Babbi, Zayde, and I think it's very important that you have a Bar Mitzvah. After that, you can decide if you want to go to Yeshiva," ordered Mom.

"I just want to go to Southampton," I explained.

The Torah hadn't saved my brother or made me famous. Mom said it was the oldest book in the world like that was a good thing. Obviously its ancient power had worn off before the Holocaust. The exuberant revelry outside my windows gave me faith. My parents hated the noise. Dad even lost control at the gaunt old lady who said "Jesus loves you," whenever she saw us as she was passing out religious pamphlets.

"Jesus doesn't love me," Dad exploded. "Don't ever shove one of those fucking pamphlets in my face again."

I wanted to get to Southampton more than ever. Mom, stressed out by the neighborhood, the humidity, and the frolicking rats, finally agreed we needed a vacation. Mom's best friend was a hippie turned elementary school principal with two daughters the same ages as my brother and me. The principal's parents had a big house in Southampton that they bought before real estate went sky high. Even if I was too poor to step foot inside my great-uncle's sprawling estate, I could at least soak up some of the limelight in the same neighborhood. There was a constant need in me for the unattainable and unknowable, surroundings so different my brain and body would be shocked into letting go. Southampton seemed a setting that would feed my desperate dreaming.

Dad stayed in the city to work in his studio. "I hate those phony people in the Hamptons anyway," he huffed. "I'm perfectly happy staying here. Good-bye." *He's always jealous*, I thought, as I lugged our heavy baggage onto the B train to Prospect Heights. Mom, Yuvi, and I were going to meet the principal at her brownstone there so we could drive out together.

The principal's daughters argued over who would get to sit in the flip-out backseat of their station wagon. Yuvi and I won in a game of Rock, Paper, Scissors, and we looked out the rear window and made faces at other drivers or held up hand-made signs that read *Honk If You're Horny*—unbeknownst to the moms.

We glided along highways touched with the orange summer sunset and stopped at a diner along the way for thick, golden onion rings, BLTs slathered in mayo, and giant lemonades. As we drove further into Long Island than I had ever gone before, the noisy city gave way to trees and small stands selling fresh produce along Route 27, where a cruising luxury convertible rushed past us. The sun-browned man and woman inside looked happy and carefree. I imagined they lived easy lives where brothers didn't choke in cheap Chinese take-out places and dads didn't try to squash celebrity aspirations.

"Can't we drive faster?" I asked Mom.

"That is dangerous and illegal," she said, handing me a box of Driscoll's strawberries. "Have a snack instead." Mom plied me with the foods I liked to fend off tantrums, tears, or questions she didn't want to answer.

The house where we stayed was a series of breezy comings and goings all summer. Iris, a beautiful forty-year-old, was staying with us. She was tall and thin with long, strawberry blonde hair and wide blue eyes that were haunted and lonely. Her husband had just died and she was looking to heal by the shore. She still wore her huge diamond wedding ring. The adults didn't tell us what her husband had died of, so we made up stories.

"I bet he was eaten by a shark," Yuvi said, biting the air to simulate carnivorous crunching.

"I bet O. J. killed him," I offered.

Since the days of Patrice, I'd thought sex was something shameful. I shuddered when I imagined strangers touching my body. When women or men complimented me on physical features—my eyes, even my growing height—I blushed and wanted to get away from them as fast as possible. I started thinking everyone wanted sex but me. Yet with Iris it was different. When I was around her I wanted to show off; my stomach tingled and my ears got hot and red. I loved the way the bones in her jaw moved when she chewed at dinner. And smelling all the bottles of lotion and perfume she kept on a shelf in the bathroom made me hard. Iris used lavender soap. I would shower after we got home from the beach, washing the sand away with the smell of her. In my eleven-year-old fantasies the soap was her hands playing with me. If I looked like the bronzed, Polo-shirted men who strolled down Main Street, smoking cigars and opening the doors of their Porsches for women who smelled like Chanel No. 5, I would have the confidence to make love to Iris. I imagined us naked on the leather backseats.

"Let me help you," she'd whisper, running her hands down my smooth chest to my penis. "You're so big for your age."

My body shuddered with delicious spasms under the steam of the shower.

I started a yard-sale buying mania among the kids, and we bullied our parents into taking us on the rounds of sales after the beach. If I couldn't afford to walk into the prim, perfect, polished, and rampantly priced air-conditioned stores on Main Street for designer duds, I could at least impress Iris with hand-me-downs, hoping the power of the previous owners lingered on the labels. We drove up endless driveways to open garages with tables covered in clothes and filled with antiques. At one sale I found an old beige suede jacket that had sheepskin trimming. Even though the sun was scorching down, something drew me to the heavy winter coat.

"This used to belong to Cat Stevens," said the regal old saleswoman as I handed her ten dollars for it.

"Oh, cool," I remarked lightly, pretending to know who Cat Stevens was.

"Really?" my mom said excitedly. "How did you get it?"

"Before he became a conservative Muslim he used to date one of my girlfriends, and one night he left his jacket in my drawing room. He never remembered to get it back."

"I love Cat Stevens," Mom gushed, fingering the coat.

"I paid for this with my allowance," I said and snatched it away from her.

I had finally found a piece of clothing that gave me status. My heart beat faster as I slipped on the jacket in the blazing Hampton heat, feeling like I was donning fame's faded, musty-smelling mantle.

As soon as we got back to the house, I downloaded Cat Steven's songs on the PC and was instantly hypnotized by his lyrics and soulful voice. My world was wild, and it was hard to get by just on my smile. I felt like part of Cat's poetry, success and glamour coursed through me. This was my chance to seduce Iris.

I ran past the cars in the driveway, stifling in Cat's heavy sheepskin coat. The sun was high and hot. I kicked up pebbles as I slid to a halt, putting one hand up over my eyes to gaze up at the guesthouse.

"Iris," I called.

There was no answer.

"Iris," I called again. "Come down. Are you there? I'm wearing Cat Steven's jacket." Sweat was pouring down my face.

I could hear the cicadas humming wildly in the trees before dying, someone mowing their lawn, a dog barking—and far away, the sea. I put my foot on the first step, lifted a hand to my mouth, and was about to call again when something stopped me. I climbed the wooden stairs up to her door.

Through the screen I saw her moving in front of a full-length mirror. There were skylights in the roof, and a dusky gold reflection fell onto her naked body. Shafts of sunlight bounced off her long, waving hair. I was fascinated by the mystery of her curves.

She moved her hands over pale pink nipples and full breasts; her pubic hair was a dark, dusty red. I started feeling hot and my vision skipped. My breathing was getting quick, my face was flushing. As I reached a hand toward her doorknob, I noticed her eyes. They were filled with tears and grief.

I went back down the stairs as quietly as I could. When I got to the bottom, I turned around.

"Iris!" I screamed. "Iris!"

She came out to stand at the top of the stairs wrapped in a silk robe.

"What is it?"

"I bought Cat Steven's jacket," I stuttered, only wanting to make her happy.

Her blank eyes slowly came into focus.

"It's beautiful," she said, smiling.

I flew back to the house over the pebbles of the drive. They were cutting into my bare feet, but I didn't feel a thing; my theater-trained lungs were singing "Wild World," ringing out every word to reach the tops of trees.

5
Becoming a Leading Man

"Rabbi Levine is a junkie," Dad told me when I asked him about the rumors flying around my Hebrew school class that the Rebbe had tried to molest a sixteen-year-old girl in the lobby of his doorman building. I was twelve and this rumor both scared and strangely excited me. And confirmed my suspicions that sex was an illicit, degrading act.

"Are you jealous that Mom likes him?" I questioned.

Rabbi Levine, the handsome head of the congregation, was mysterious. Mom had gone on a blind date with him back in Great Neck when she was still getting her master's in comparative literature at Queen's College.

"One of the ex-hookers at my job used to sell him heroin," Dad replied. "They'd shoot it together, then she'd tie him up and whip him. Just goes to show you how hypocritical all these religious nuts are." Dad put a topcoat of glaze on the Seder plate that Babbi and Zayde had commissioned from him. As a Bar Mitzvah present for me, my parents were painting a front room of our apartment beige and deep red, so I could move out of the room I shared with Yuvi into my own private space.

"You can pick any one of my masks you want to hang in your new room," Dad offered.

I had always coveted the colorful characters he hung high up on his studio walls, looming down at me like all-powerful gods as I grew up. I pointed to a woman clutching a fat crescent moon in her mouth, face covered in shining stars.

"I want the moon lady," I said.

"Moon lady?" Dad shook with laughter, "That's a double dildo."

In horror I realized my mistake. The curving shape she clutched between her lips ended in two bulbous cockheads. How was I supposed to become a man when my father's special art world was devoted to dicks? Not just one, or a few, but penises with two heads? I even noticed a painting of a black man whose prick morphed into a giant python, wrapping endlessly around his legs.

Spending my Sundays in Hebrew school learning prayers to a God I didn't believe in and who wouldn't help speed up the process of puberty was a waste of time. Mom bribed Yuvi and me into going by taking us out for lunch after at the Big Enchilada, our favorite fix for spicy *Traif* (definitely, deliciously non-kosher) ground-beef burritos.

"The only reason I'm having a Bar Mitzvah is to make you happy," I told Mom.

"And for the money," Yuvi reminded me.

"Maybe you'll learn to see the beauty in Judaism when you study your Torah portion with Cantor Elliot," Mom said hopefully.

Cantor Elliot was cross-eyed and opened his mouth so wide when he sang that I thought his throat must be full of inhaled *yarmulkes*. I thirsted for sex, fame, and drama—not davening, the endless moans of religious men as they keened and dipped their heads, bowing to the Torah and to a God who was invisible to me.

After we got back from Southampton, I convinced Mom to dry clean Cat Stevens' coat with her work clothes in preparation for my Bar Mitzvah. I thought it looked even more impressive on a wire hanger wrapped in plastic and hung in my closet to wait comfortably for cold weather—though I really wanted to show it off for my first day of junior high. My parents and I were ecstatic when I got accepted to the Clinton School for Writers and Artists in Chelsea. I had listed it as my number-one choice on the Board of Education form.

"It's the kind of place I wish my parents would have let me go to," Dad told me. "They never understood how important it is to encourage artistic growth."

"Can I have a backpack?" I asked.

"You can use one of my old artist tote bags," Dad said.

As the new kid in a nicer neighborhood, I couldn't get away with carrying my notebooks to school in an old, striped Osh Kosh shoulder bag or one of the battered black artists' totes Dad insisted "got the job done." He surprised me a few nights later by announcing that he'd take Yuvi and me shopping for satchels on Broadway at my favorite store, Ground Zero. As soon as I had done clearing our family dinner dishes off the table, we set off through the heavy late summer night.

"I want a Jansport too," Yuvi said, tugging on Dad's hand as I picked out an alpine green one.

"Demands, demands! You're in third grade," my father muttered. "When you graduate you can get one too."

Yuvi kicked dead leaves as we walked home through Sarah Delano Roosevelt Park. I hugged my new Jansport to my chest, relishing the luxury. I was excited about starting school with people who didn't know me. It was a chance for reinvention and to get away from hood friends, who'd get into fistfights and tease me in loud, angry voices. There were so many people I could decide to be. Just then I spotted a small leather knapsack sitting alone on a bench, partially hidden by some shrubs and empty beer bottles.

"Dad, go see what's in there," I pointed, curious, but not wanting to get my hands dirty. My father, always eager to dumpster dive, unzipped a pocket of the bag and crisp green dollar bills spilled out. He looked around nervously into the night that was lit by orange streetlamps.

"This has to be drug money," he muttered, unzipping a smaller pocket also filled with bills.

"Can we keep it?" Yuvi asked.

"Finders keepers, losers weepers," my father said. "But don't tell anyone we found it. If this is what I think it is, we could be tracked down and killed."

"Hide it in my new bag," I said, thinking quickly. I was ecstatic that I had found so much money. I liked the danger. It was an early Bar Mitzvah present—hard cash my parents couldn't take 90 percent of. I could buy cool new cowboy boots to match Cat's jacket. I'd get my brother a TV, fancy earrings for Mom, new paints for Dad.

"Close your eyes," my father told Mom when we got home. She was wearing a lacey turquoise nightgown, ready to go to sleep. Yuvi and I giggled as he dumped what seemed like millions of fresh dollar bills all over their bedroom floor.

Mom gasped. "Where did you . . ."

"I found it in the park," I said proudly, jumping on the bed and hugging her.

"Let's count it," Yuvi suggested.

The four of us sat on their oriental rug counting out stacks of ten singles each for an hour.

"Three thousand four hundred and eighty seven dollars," Dad shouted as he counted out the last of the bills.

"I'm rich," I screamed.

My parents exchanged looks.

"This money doesn't belong to you," Dad said.

"You're a liar! You said finders keepers," I yelled at him.

"This from the boy who begged for a backpack that his nice father sacrificed his studio time and hard-earned money for," Dad said and shook a finger at me.

"You'll get plenty of presents for your Bar Mitzvah," Mom answered and tried to smooth my hair as if to quell the rage for revenge already rising behind my brows. I pulled away.

"That's the only reason the kid is getting Bar Mitzvahed. This cash is going to household improvements," my father announced. "If it's not counterfeit."

"I'll be following right behind you on my bike," he reassured me the next day as I boarded the M15 bus for my first day of school.

"I don't care," I said. I was nervous about meeting richer kids who hadn't grown up in my bad neighborhood, and I was angry that he had confiscated my cash.

"God, your breath smells sour," he replied. "Must be the anxiety."

I glared at him pedaling alongside my bus while I compulsively chewed a whole pack of Wrigley's Spearmint gum and the Lower East Side disappeared behind us. Chelsea was filled with bedraggled drag queens. A bar across the street from my new school had blacked-out windows and was called "Rawhide."

Transferring in a year late, I didn't fit in with my fellow seventh graders, who had already bonded in sixth grade's mandatory ballroom dancing class. I couldn't wear Cat's jacket yet, didn't have the money I found to impress my new classmates, and couldn't even tell anyone about it for fear my family would be murdered. Like the neighborhood, my new school was colorful and loud, but not in the brash way of the Lower East Side. There was a comely order to Chelsea that impressed me. My fellow students seemed more confident in their clothes and place in the world. They laughed, without fear, walking through the streets.

At lunchtime, I sat alone. I glimpsed a girl giggling through the crowds. The fueled chatter faded and she swung her blonde-streaked hair over her shoulder in slow motion. When she caught my eye, I shyly turned away, feeling like I wasn't good enough to be looking. I stared down at my too-tattered royal blue Converse high tops. Then two Doc Martens planted themselves in front of me.

"I'm Morgan. What's your name?" asked the girl I had been staring at, grinning down at me.

"Hazak," I muttered.

"How bizarre. I like it. Hey, want to be Mulder to my Scully?" she asked.

I nodded. I suddenly loved the *X-Files*.

"Come on," she grabbed my hand and we tore down the school corridor away from the teachers with our fingers pointed into makeshift guns.

Two weeks later, I took the 6 train uptown to meet Morgan's cold Catholic mom, who made me uncomfortable. It didn't help that she was married to a loud Jew who walked into their beige living room announcing that he sold fabric wholesale to JC Penney. I was afraid to tell Morgan about my upcoming Bar Mitzvah, sure if she found out my Hebrew clan was just as crazy as her father, she'd dump me.

I knew Babbi and Zayde would disapprove of my new half-shiksa girlfriend with WASP-y headshots. Morgan was best friends with a chubby sidekick named Melon who wrote dark poetry about death that made everyone in our English class cry. My poems, stories, and drawings also drew attention and as always, became my way of making friends. No one cared if I was awkward or soft spoken, or given to bouts of cruelty and perversion, as long as I could create escapes with my art and words. Also, because of my Dad's influence, the popular demand of my classmates, and the need to feed my own growing sexual fantasies, my drawings were often of our teachers in various states of undress, legs spread wide, sex organs depicted to the best of my limited knowledge. It was rumored that our principal had a dossier full of my confiscated drawings. This edge of wickedness, with its level of notoriety, if not fame, added to my appeal

I felt like I had to treat Morgan and Melon as an inseparable pair. Morgan stole Excedrin from the A&P, and Melon told me they cut their arms with thumbtacks. When I asked Morgan where she got the wounds, she gave me her toothpaste commercial smile and said, "My dog scratched me."

At twelve, on my way to becoming a man, I thought I could save her like my parents saved their patients. I diagnosed her with low self-esteem.

The same week I discovered Morgan's cutting, Melon started calling me and we wound up spending hours on the phone together. She told me that her mom was a well-known fashion photographer. Her surly dad was terminally ill with some disease I'd never heard of that she'd inherited. I snuck into the bathroom that Dad had papered with Wrigley's gum wrappers from the gum I had been chewing obsessively. With my parents' cordless in hand, I quietly rubbed Mom's raspberry-scented hand lotion on my stiff prick, pretending my fingers were Melon's fingers.

"I really love you," she blurted, as I dry spasmed, muscles contracting.

Before I could answer her, Melon said, "Morgan is calling me on the other line. Hold on, babe."

She got back on with a heavy sob. "She wants you to be her date for our prom at the dude ranch."

"I can take both of you," I offered. "No one has to feel lonely."

"No, you can't." Melon sobbed.

"Then tell Morgan yes," I said.

By eighth grade Morgan and I had gone to the junior high prom together, and when she was offered a starring role in a commercial for snack bars, she got me a part as an extra in a crowd scene. I took a bus uptown to meet her in a school cafeteria for the shoot. There were giant lights everywhere, and the director's assistant and grips were running around, clutching cups of coffee. It felt amazing to be thrust back into the busy Hollywood world I thought had passed me by.

"You're here," Morgan gushed, as she kissed my cheek. She looked older in makeup and more beautiful than Christina Ricci, my number-one matinee crush. Her nose was impossibly pointed, almost as if shaved off at the tip, and her large brown eyes slanted slightly at the corners. She looked delicate, foreign, lost, and wholesome all at once. Like some famous imp given to flannel, poetry, and professions of love that left my heart feeling stronger than forever.

I watched her go over her lines, while I tried to get attention during my crowd scene. I flailed my arms around and let out huge belly laughs, slapping my thigh, thinking I was a much better actor than the crowd of bored-looking, acne-covered extras.

"Would you mind not moving? You're an eyesore in the background," the production assistant hissed at me, before hurrying back behind the cameras. Ron Howard had shaken my hand. Didn't they understand that I knew what I was doing?

Morgan was always dropped off at school and picked up by a town car, and she would wave to me out the back window as she sped off. Her lavender bedroom in her parents' house on 88th Street and Third Avenue was plastered with pictures of Kurt Cobain and Absolut ads. She'd been a child model featured in a JC Penney catalog and was an aspiring actress. I was sure if I was famous too, she'd love me.

"Sometimes I think my parentals wouldn't notice if I disappeared," she confided as we lay on her purple carpet, Kurt looking back at us.

"My parents would notice. They're way too involved," I said, reaching for her hand.

If I could perform the ancient prayers of my tribe perfectly at my upcoming Bar Mitzvah, I'd get money to fly us to Hollywood. No agents were calling me, but Mom's synagogue on 12th Street and University Place was—and at least they had a stage.

In June, Grandpa Morris flew in from Springfield, Illinois, with my great-aunt Dorrie, who had her own suite at the Sixth Avenue Hilton and kept her diamond earrings locked in the safe.

"I can't believe with all the money that bastard has, his only present to you was a fucking *tallis*," my father fumed, after Grandpa Morris presented me with the tasseled garment.

"What an asshole," I agreed, following my father's lead, blaming Grandpa Morris for all of my father's disappointments.

"Don't worry, I won't let him give a speech at the celebration," Dad reassured me.

I was excited to be on the *bimah*, with hundreds of friends and relatives looking on. Mom and Zayde had helped me with Hebrew pronunciation. I soared through the *V'ahavta*, prayer relishing the theatrical echo of my voice in the temple. The Torah portion I had been assigned *to read* was about Korach, a Jew who rebelled against Moses while their tribe wandered in the desert after exile from Egypt and was swallowed by the earth. I secretly feared I would be punished for reciting the ancient passages just for presents and attention and not because I believed in them. I noticed Rabbi Levine kept nodding off. Suspecting him of shooting up made me feel better about my own sacrilegious agenda. As I placed the heavy scrolls wrapped in a velvet cover back in the arc, Rabbi Levine turned to me.

"Go up there and deliver your semen," he whispered.

"What?" I blushed, looking out at the audience, but I was the only one who had heard his heroin-addled slip.

"Go deliver your sermon," he corrected himself, quickly retiring to a chair hidden by a podium. After my speech, Zayde lectured that Judaism was the most precious gift of all to bestow on a Bar Mitzvah and congratulated me.

"I'd like to say a few words," Grandpa Morris said as he stood up from the first row of benches.

I looked at my father. He grimaced and shrugged while Grandpa Morris got on stage and placed a firm hand on my shoulder.

"This is the part about Moses you didn't hear today." His voice crackled through the mic. "When the Jews stopped at Mount Sinai and he went to the top, God offered him the commandments. 'How much are they?' Moshe asked. 'They're free,' God replied. 'In that case, I'll take ten,' said the cheapskate." Grandpa Morris' chuckle reverberated through the silent synagogue.

The humiliation was worth the proceeds. My take away after my parents had snatched their 90 percent for my college fund was five hundred dollars, more than I'd ever had in my life. I splurged on wide-leg Kik Wear jeans from a store near Canal Street called Yellow Rat Bastard, relishing the name when questioned by concerned adults about the origin of my pants, which swept the sidewalks around me, drenched to the knees in rain. I also bought a black choker with a cross on it for Morgan, a crucifix being more meaningful than a Star of David.

After I became a man by Jewish law, Melon invited Morgan and me to visit her parents' cottage in upstate New York and go to a Goo Goo Dolls concert. I had never been to a concert before and the thought of being close to rock stars with my up-and-coming girlfriend made me feel like a VIP.

"I think Morgan is a snob," my father informed me, when I asked if I could go on the trip.

"Mixed sleepovers are not okay. You're too old for that now," Mom explained.

"Babbi let you fly to Israel when you were sixteen," I reminded her.

"I was three years older than you and very interested in Judaism," she argued.

"You were a hippie who wanted to run away from your mom," I argued back. "Besides, you said after my Bar Mitzvah I could start making my own decisions."

"As long as it's strictly chaperoned and you don't sleep in the same room," she decided.

"Make sure he doesn't get anyone pregnant," Dad quipped to Melon's parents as I loaded my bags into their car, my thirteen-year-old face burning with embarrassment. Already too tall for my age, but still with rings of pudge around my middle and acne creeping in swaths over my shoulders like some shameful shawl, my desires were tempered with the feeling that I was monstrous. Only my eyes, the pale blue openings that had invited fame and disaster my whole life, redeemed me. People praised and flirted with their openness, their light, and their "watchfulness"—a quality I couldn't control. Morgan and Melon both sunk into those eyes and loved me more for them.

The Red Hot Chili Pepper's "Scartissue" came on the radio as we left the fast-paced buzz of the city behind us. Morgan and I discreetly sucked each other's fingers in the dark backseat. I felt awful going further with her while Melon sat quietly next to us, big and sad, staring out the window, lips moving to the music. Her parents looked straight ahead without saying anything as the car zoomed through the night, headlights illuminating the grey road in front of us.

When we finally got to the country house, Morgan and I hopped out of the car. The sky was filled with bright stars that shone clearly with no city smog to veil them.

"There's a pond in back," Melon said.

Morgan and I exchanged theatrical love-struck looks.

"We're going to go check it out. Carry our bags inside, Melon," Morgan instructed, pulling me around the back of the dark house. I saw lights come on in the cabin and then the unmistakably round shape of Melon standing on a wooden balcony, her silhouette deeper than the darkness. The stars reflected in the pond. The night was full of throaty frog calls. The country was like a big soundstage designed for a cheesy love scene. It was the perfect place to have my first real kiss. Morgan led me to the edge of the still, black pool filled with pinpricks of light. She bent by the shore, tearing off a piece of long grass and tucking it between her teeth.

"What are you doing?" I asked.

"Come get it," she said, overly seductive.

I reached for her lips with my hands.

"No," she pinned them behind my back.

I was turned on that she was in control. Bending my body closer to hers, I leaned in and imagined our first lip-lock would be like Leonardo DiCaprio and Claire Danes in Baz Luhrman's *Romeo+Juliet*. Morgan bit my tongue, then licked me from my chin to my nose. Her breath was scared and hot, and her tongue left a trail that smelled like the floating debris in the bottom of an empty jar of pickles.

"What was that?" I blurted.

"A kiss," Morgan said and pushed me.

"Maybe you should chew some Winterfresh first, the next time, like me," I said.

She started to cry. Horrified, I tried to hold her in my arms, but she pushed them away.

"I'm sorry," I said, smoothing her hair back from her forehead like Mom did to me when I was young and woke from nightmares sobbing. She looked up at me then, eyes wet as the pond behind us.

"No, I'm sorry," she said, "I don't love you as much as you love me. I just don't."

The next night was our rock show finale before returning to New York. I was revved up about going to see the girl's favorite band, the Goo Goo Dolls, at a local stadium. I didn't like their music, but it was a chance to bask in borrowed rock 'n' roll glory at the footlights.

"Let's go up front," I suggested, wanting to be as close to the famous musicians as possible.

"Duh—mosh pit!" Morgan screamed, grabbing my hand and dragging me through the crowd of scary-looking sunburnt teens in trucker hats and flannel cut off shirts—right up to the towering security guards who flanked the stage.

"Rock out, rock out," hundreds of voices around us chanted. People started lighting up fat joints and the air was thick with sweet smoke. I started to feel lightheaded, and famous by proximity. I wished I could knock the security guards out of the way and jump onstage to revel in the desire and awe the mob had for these larger than life, eyeliner-wearing '90s heartthrobs.

The Goo Goo Dolls rushed on and the stadium lights blared, making red, white, and blue spotlights zigzag over the shouting crowd. The blast of lead singer Johnny Resnick's guitar made my spine bend. His short, androgynous bandmate Robby jumped around like a gargantuan garden gnome.

"Are you okay?" Morgan asked.

"I'm a little hot," I said, grinning uncontrollably, the grinding people around me morphing into one tumultuous mass of dangerous light and color. A wide older woman with a scraggly, grey mullet rammed into me.

"Watch it, ya little shit!" she yelled, as someone on her other side yanked her back and the mob swallowed her.

"I need to get out of here," I said, feeling claustrophobic.

"Don't be such a wimp." Morgan glared at me.

"He needs to sit down." Melon said and faced Morgan.

I turned away before they could say anything else, reeling through the endless sea of fans and choking on the secondhand smoke.

When I finally got out of the hot-boxed mosh pit and tried to get onto the bleachers, a double-chinned guy with a blonde buzz cut eating a sausage asked to see my ticket. I realized Melon had it; there was no way I could go back.

"Can't sit without it," Buzz cut said chewing.

I skulked away to a shadowy part of the walkway that ran between the seats and the open, wild crush of groupies and sat down behind a garbage can.

The familiar smell of the gutter made me homesick. I was stuck in upstate New York with two girls who no longer loved me, listening to the Goo Goo Dolls next to the trash, stoned for the first time and starting to cry.

"Did you have a good trip?" Mom asked when I got home. My unfinished new bedroom was still covered in drop cloths, and thick plastic sheets smothered the wood floors.

"It was kind of confusing," I confessed, throwing myself on the living room couch, where I had been temporarily sleeping for almost a month while Dad's friend painted—sometimes in just his disgusting tight, white underwear. I knew the drug money from the bag I had discovered in the park was paying him.

"I'm so glad you feel like you can talk to me, sweetie," Mom smiled. "I got you this book while you were away, to help you understand puberty."

She handed me a blue copy of *What's Happening To My Body?* I anxiously flipped through it when she left the room. There was a diagram depicting male genitals in various states of development. I slipped my hand down the front of my pants, feeling my growing penis and decided generously that I was at least up to figure four. I quickly flipped pages until I came to the chapter about girls. This also had an illustrated diagram, except it was of the whole body, including breasts budding slowly into fullness. I felt myself get hard as I wondered what Morgan looked like. I pushed my pants down around my ankles, stroking myself and hoping I was old enough to spurt cum.

"Hazak?" I heard Mom's voice in the darkened living room.

I grabbed a pillow, shoving it over my throbbing hard-on, just as her face, fringed with dark, wavy hair peered around the corner of a shelf that was sectioning off my sleeping space.

"How's the book?" She asked.

"Really informative, thanks. I'm learning a lot," I squeaked in reply, hoping she couldn't see me blushing.

"It's so dark in here. How can you read?" Mom asked.

"The streetlamps," I said, pointing to the orange glow from the security lights of the projects across the street slanting in through our front windows.

"Well, goodnight sweetie, love you," Mom said, making kissy noises as she walked toward the back of the house.

I waited, counting slowly to one hundred, then reopened the book, but now, all I could look at were the pictures of fully developed women with large, dangling breasts and fat, bushy vaginas. The dangerous brush with Mom made me even more aroused than before. As I shot my first sperm over my stomach, I hazily realized I would probably have to analyze this for years.

6
Curtain Call

Al Pacino, Jennifer Aniston, Adrien Brody, Sarah Michelle Gellar.
I was desperate to start at the famous LaGuardia High School of Music
& Art and Performing Arts, whose alumni list left me starstruck. I spent
the months before my entrance exam preparing a portfolio with Dad.
I looked for hints of his loud, colorful style seeping into my sketches
and scratched out lines that looked too much like his. We spent hours
together in his studio while he gave me pointers on passing the notori-
ously tough test.

"The face needs more contours," he commented, taking my hand
in his as he taught me how to shade above the temples and on either
side of the nose. Grateful, I thought he was finally backing my dreams.
Since LaGuardia was a public high school, anyone could apply, but the
teachers selected only a few students based on their work and a two-
hour drawing assessment.

"They're not looking for perfection, they're looking for promise,"
Dad reassured me when I got stressed out, squirting black paint across
an overworked canvass. In my private pages, I scribbled naked women
with Pamela Anderson-size tits having sex with muscular men, pictur-
ing the pussy I wasn't getting. All the dicks were bigger than Dad's penis drawings.

On test day, I took the B train to the giant brown brick building
that took up an entire block across from Lincoln Center on the corner
of 66th Street and Amsterdam Avenue. My adrenaline was pumping as

a student volunteer led a herd of hopefuls to a huge art studio on the top floor. We were assigned seats and had to draw an upperclassman forced to model. He posed sulkily in the middle of the room, a tall creature with shaggy, bright orange hair and green bellbottoms. I had never seen a boy dress like this, except in old movies from the '60s. My shock and curiosity were clear in the messy lines of my sketch and were still boldly present in the deep shadows I drew in our next test: a still life from imagination. I went over my portfolio with a teacher who paged through it with a blank expression and nodded for the next kid.

"There's going to be another artist in the family," my father exclaimed when I got my acceptance letter to LaGuardia. I loved Dad's approval, but he had hijacked my moment. Suddenly I wasn't pleased.

"I don't want to be an artist like you Dad," I said, without thinking.

"Do you know how hard I work to put clothes on your back and food on the table? You think life is so easy you can just decide to be an artist and that's that? Well, guess what, mister, you better start studying something practical like social work because I'm not footing your fucking bills forever," Dad said, then headed downstairs to his studio like he always did before he completely lost his temper.

Though Dad worked hard to contain the rages that still ran through him, our clashing ambitions brought them rushing out. When I brought his wishes to life, I was rewarded with his endless praise and admiration, with hours spent side by side working in the warm lights of his studio as we listened to NPR. But when my stubborn streaks of independence were revealed, my father suddenly switched into a wounded man, responding by attacking, abandoning, and threatening to take away the one thing I wanted most: his love.

An easy way for me to slip into a different persona, to seem like something more interesting than an ungrateful, unhappy boy was to dye my hair. I admired my new Manic Panic Bad Boy Blue color in the mirror later that night. Dad tapped on the bathroom door.

"I planned a surprise family vacation so we can bond before you turn into even more of an obnoxious, rebellious teen," he said, sounding pleased with himself. "You're going through that stage where you're feeling your oats."

"I can't go anywhere. I just got back from a Goo Goo Dolls concert and I need to get ready for LaGuardia," I said. Dad had worked hard to help me get into my dream school. Now, I feared he was purposefully foiling preparations for the creative training I craved.

"I already rented the cabin," he replied. "We'll be overlooking a lake twenty times the size of Manhattan, in Moosehead, Maine, population 2,500."

"That's the same amount of people that will be in my high school, but trapped in the middle of nowhere." I quickly did the dismal math.

"Tommy Hilfiger does photo shoots there, and besides, the country air will do you good," said Dad, who had fled the plains of the Midwest to pursue his dreams in the polluted streets of New York. I wondered if my father's mention of Tommy Hilfiger was his way of manipulating me, or maybe he too gravitated toward destinations where the rich and famous lived and the possibility of discovery dangled.

In the car ride up, nine-year-old Yuvi and I forced our parents to keep the radio tuned to Z100, which played Vitamin C's "Graduation (Friends Forever)." I bobbed my head to the beat, letting the wind from the open window whip back my blue hair. Yuvi sat beside me, engrossed with the screenplay he had been writing in his notebook. All my brother wanted to do was make a movie about a crime fighting superhero named after his weapon of choice, The Plunger.

"The main villain will be a half-man, half-cat called Mr. Kibbles N' Bits," he explained.

"He should wear a suit and top hat," I suggested.

As the city fell away behind us, the scenery turned to trees and the radio, which had been playing Santana and Rob Thomas's "Smooth," crackled and faded into twangy country music.

"Fix it," I grumbled, fingering the black-studded wristband Morgan had stolen for me from a St. Mark's Place punk store. I unsnapped it and stuffed it between the seats of our Honda rental. I had lost her love. After our disastrous weekend getaway, I felt like high school would do nothing but force us further apart.

"Don't you dare touch it!" Dad barked, as Mom reached for the radio dial. "I hate driving. No distractions. Every one just calm down."

"Go faster," said Yuvi.

After we turned off the flat, empty highway, we took winding roads to a small town. Cruising down Main Street, I saw a diner, a gas station, and a head shop whose window was filled with bongs and tie-dyed T-shirts. Bored-looking teens loitered on a corner and one of their faces looked like it had been ripped up and sewn back on. I wondered if there were bears in the pine trees and if they had mauled him.

"We're lost in the fucking woods," Dad announced, as we drove in circles on the dirt roads outside town limits.

"There's a convenience store. Why don't you ask for directions?" Mom pointed to a wooden shack by the side of the road.

"Did they tell you where Tommy shoots his ads?" I asked when Dad got back in the rental car.

"No, they gave me directions to our cabin." He put the keys in the ignition. "They said if they were in Times Square they'd be just as lost as us, but at least in Maine there aren't any Negroes. We're all the same color. Good thing I didn't tell them we were Jews." Dad laughed nervously, trying to joke as he quickly revved the car into action.

"That's horrible," Mom gasped.

"What if everyone in the world was a robot except for one man?" Yuvi asked me. "And one day he cut open his brother's skin while he was sleeping and instead of blood and bones, there were machine parts?"

"It would make a great movie," I said.

"I'll make that one after I release The Plunger," he announced.

"Why don't you make one about racist rednecks who find out a family of Jews are staying in one of their lakeside cabins and decide to murder them?" I suggested.

Mom shook her head. "That's not funny, Hazak."

When we finally came across the cabin, nestled in trees I could not name, the strangeness of our surroundings settled on me. A wood stove sat in our new living room and a massive stuffed Moose head with antlers spreading like angel wings loomed above it. This seemed furthest from the Lower East Side I had ever been. The silence scared me and I unpacked quickly, eager to place my few familiar possessions around my small bedroom in an attempt to make it more my own.

"We're going to a special restaurant," Dad crowed as we bumped along dirt roads in the dark. "It's a farm and everything is grown right there, very exclusive."

Every few feet there were yellow signs warning of moose crossings. I imagined vicious, antlered animals. Between bears, moose, and car crashes, I was petrified I'd be disfigured before I could start school with kids I imagined were already singing on Broadway in September.

"Can I get you anything to drink?" our waiter asked as we sat down at an authentic wooden table.

"Since we're splurging, I'll have a dry vodka martini," Dad ordered. I was surprised because both my parents were strict nondrinkers. I had never seen my father even tipsy.

"Can I have one?" I asked hopefully, wanting to see how far I could push.

"You can have a sip of mine," he said.

"I want a sip too," Yuvi decided.

"Neither of them is having a sip. Absolutely not," said Mom.

The dining room was nearly empty, but I approved of the well-dressed couples eating and throwing back giant glasses of red wine by candlelight. When it came, Dad drank his martini in two gulps, wincing like it was medicine. As he chewed big mouthfuls of arugula salad he started laughing hysterically. Yuvi and I exchanged worried glances.

"Did you ever hear about the Native American tribe the Fucka-wees?" Dad chortled, salad dressing running down his chin. Mom laughed nervously.

"No," I said.

"They got their name because they were lost in the forest one day and the chief screamed 'Where the fuckawee?'" Dad burst into uncontrollable laughter. The elegant diners shot pointed looks in our direction as I blushed and sunk into my seat.

I left the dinner table early, hoping I might run into a modeling scout on the sprawling grounds of the farm. I kicked around an old soccer ball abandoned in the parking lot and made my way down to the wooden dock where a tan old man in a small motorboat was smoking a cigar; the dusk, sending teasing orange strips of sun over the gentle water, matched his burning ember through the growing dark.

"Excuse me, does Tommy Hilfiger do photo shoots here?" I asked.

"The son of a bitch flew out in his private chopper last week," he replied, glaring up at me. "You know him, kid?"

"Not personally."

"Good. Better not to get mixed up with them fancy folk," he advised, his face softening.

When Dad sobered up enough to drive us back to our cabin, the impenetrable country night had fallen.

"Want to take a walk?" he asked me as I slammed the door of our car.

"Sure," I said, happy to be close to him, just the two of us.

We strolled along the edge of the lake as I kicked stones and listened to them hitting the water.

"I know this isn't the most exciting place," my father said.

"It's fun." I lied.

"The only time I got drunk was in high school. I was an intellectual in Chicago, where we were living at the time, and it made me nerdy," he chuckled. "I didn't really have many friends."

I looked up to see if Dad was still tipsy, but I couldn't see his face. We were both covered in night. He wasn't slurring or falling down like the drunks in our neighborhood.

"I had a crush on the most popular girl in school," he said. "I blacked out on her lawn in the middle of our senior prom party screaming, 'Fuck me, Peggy! Fuck me!' All night long, and I don't even remember. My friends had to carry me home, and when I came to my mother was standing over me shaking her head and saying 'dirty penny.'"

I laughed. I wondered why he hid this loud, crazy side behind his sober social worker persona, but felt like if I asked any questions, he wouldn't keep telling me his secrets.

"It's not funny. It was horrible. Alcohol is dangerous. I regret it to this day." My father frowned.

"It's not a big deal, Dad," I said.

"All my childhood, my mother told me I was ugly," he continued as if he hadn't heard me. "She'd go into fits and pick up the phone, threatening to call an adoption agency to take me away. What kind of mother would do that to her child? Morris was gone fighting World War II when I was little and my grandmother never did anything to stop it."

I wanted to grab at him in the darkness and hug him. I remembered Patrice and how angry and scared I was when no one saved me.

"Do I seem alright to you?" he asked.

"Of course you do," I said quickly.

I knew he wasn't. He had raised me to spot early psychological symptoms like drinking and reaching out for help. But I needed him to be strong for both of us. I felt if he wasn't, I'd buckle under the weight of his sadness. A pain, I now knew he had carried around for all those years.

"That's okay. You're in your own world. It's the start of your Oedipal phase." Dad sounded hurt.

"What's that?" I asked.

"It basically means you want to cut off my penis and have sex with your mother," Dad said. "But really it's about asserting yourself as a man."

"Well, I don't want to be Oedipal." I said, reaching for his hand. "I love you."

"There will always be deep fear and jealousy between a father and son. Let's go inside." He turned away.

The picture windows in our rented cabin's living room were completely black, making it impossible to see out. The lack of streetlamps and city noise made me feel exposed. When I finally fell asleep I had a nightmare that my father was wearing a flannel shirt and chasing me through the woods with a chainsaw. "I'll kill you fancy folk!" he screamed after me as I tore through the underbrush.

In the morning I woke up with a boner. I quickly hid my crotch in the blankets, thinking about what Dad had told me. I was the only late sleeper in our family, and I could hear my brother and parents already in the kitchen cooking and laughing. My father seemed fine now, but I feared he saw my growing maleness as a threat in his house. I would never do violent sex things to him or Mom. I wanted to have my own wife and children, not ruin and rape my parents. Yet I suddenly feared I did need to irrevocably wound them to be free.

I went out onto our porch and leaned over the wooden railing. It would be better to hurt myself than Dad. Wind blew off the grey lake and I could see the towering shapes of islands in the mist. The view frightened me and made me feel more alone. Recognizing my father's wounds opened my own. I was poison, especially to my family. There was an easy end that would guarantee at least a few newspaper headlines.

I slowly walked down the steps toward the lake. I waded into the freezing water up to my ankles, looking out to where the small waves got rough. I knelt down and put my face under the water. It was even colder than I expected and my skin shriveled in shock. Water went up my nose, making me choke. I came back up sputtering.

My family was crowded over a heated game of Scrabble when I returned and made my dripping grand entrance. I imagined rushing into their arms and screaming that I was a new person.

"Why are you all wet?" my father asked, barely glancing up from the board.

"I tried to drown myself in the lake," I said.

"You're so dramatic," Mom laughed.

"Bingo! Seven-letter word!" Dad shouted.

Only Yuvi shot me a concerned look.

"I'll give you a part in *The Plunger*," he promised.

Suicide was too Kurt Cobain. Besides, I had to start high school.

7
I Want to Live Forever

"You are all rising stars," my new principal droned into a microphone my first day at LaGuardia—the high school immortalized in the movie Fame. I wondered why he looked so uncool: a short man who was stuffed into an outdated brown suit and sported thick glasses and a toupee. I glanced nervously around at the masses of talented freshman who'd eagerly stormed the building and herded into a giant auditorium. Dyed hair abounded, from electric lava red to enchanted forest green. There were punks with safety pins stuck through their noses, Goths with black shoelaces tied around their necks, rich kids in studied vintage carrying designer bags, and a Chinese boy in full drag with a silver wig and blue contacts. It was clear that the administration expected all students to become boldfaced names on marquees, proving the school's prowess.

In my first period watercolor class, I sat next to a girl with a long face and curvy body. Hunched over her paints, eyes covered in her hot pink hair, she seemed rough around the edges, like me, with a tough sadness in her green eyes.

"I think I know you from somewhere. Where did you go to middle school?" she asked, as we shared paints.

"Clinton School for Writers and Artists," I said, showing off.

"I love artsy boys. I'm Cecelia," she said, giggling.

Cecelia also loved photography and spent hours in the school's darkroom. After we became friends, we would meet halfway between our parents' houses on a stoop next to the Polish butcher on Seventh Street and First Avenue. She took me around Soho, snapping away photos with me as her model. She coyly convinced me to hold the cigarettes she smoked when she took my photos, though I didn't take drags. The swirling smoke around my face added something undeniably seductive to the images when I saw them developed, looking gritty underneath their chemical gloss.

Cecelia told me she loved Fleetwood Mac and my Cat Stevens' jacket. She got stoned and puffed menthol cigarettes.

"Once you start smoking weed, you become a junkie," I said, repeating my parents' party line.

"That's bullshit," she shot back.

"You shouldn't hurt yourself," I responded. I grabbed her and held on as tight as I could.

"If you don't want to smoke with me, fine. But if I do it's none of your fucking business," she said and pulled away, lighting up another Newport.

"I'll hurt myself too, then," I answered, grabbing her cigarette away and taking a long puff that left me light-headed as she leaned in to kiss me, nicotine and menthol tingling on our tongues.

"Go ahead. It's sexy," she murmured.

Tired of jerking off to illustrations of naked fourteen-year-old girls sprouting pubic hair in my already worn copy of *What's Happening To My Body?*, I stumbled across Mom's teenage diaries hidden in a dusty crate on top of a bookshelf in the new room I'd gotten as a Bar Mitzvah present. The room used to be Mom's office and she still kept some things stored among my *Danger Girl* comic books and baggy jeans. The old journals were filled with poems and pressed flowers. I was shocked to come across her description of "an encounter" with the bearded, older boy in bellbottoms whose picture had been pasted under the entry. I instantly lost my own erection.

I had never thought my mom's seemingly innocent suburban adolescence hid a secret wild child. I was impressed. I decided I wanted to lose my virginity immediately. Dad made paintings of wild orgies on disheveled barroom Billiard tables, and now I knew Mom had been a young siren. I couldn't think of a better way to claim my manhood than to have sex sooner than my supposedly celibate teen mom coming of age in the '70s. That wasn't Oedipal at all.

⚘

Cecelia gave me my first blow job at fourteen in my parent's roof garden, overlooking lower Manhattan. The September sun was shining and making dizzying orange lights dance behind my eyelids from between the twin towers. She whispered, "I'll only do it if you don't look."

Afterwards, I slid my fingers inside her, then fed her small, fermenting wine grapes growing on a gnarled vine. I had stolen scraps of romantic scenes from movies, and this one was straight from Christian Slater's character in *Bed of Roses*—seducing the girl with my wild arbor of a roof in a city made of metal and glass.

"What were you doing up there?" my father questioned, when I came down two hours later.

"Just talking with Cecelia," I blushed.

"Don't you have schoolwork? I want you coming straight home from now on. I don't like that girl. She never says hello to me," Dad said.

"She's just shy," I said, defending her.

"I don't care. She's rude," he snapped.

I slammed the door to my room, furiously analyzing the situation. Cecelia had never even met her father, an ex-cokehead who'd fled to Florida before she was born. Her mom, a lawyer, had remarried a security guard who drank nonalcoholic O'Doul's beer. They'd spoil her with shopping sprees at Wet Seal then ignore her, instead lavishing love on her younger half sister. Cecelia's unhappy family history fascinated me. In it, I saw a chance to save her, to bring understanding and happiness into her life. It was a powerful feeling to think that I could be the source of her healing, and also that in some ways our complicated and intense family struggles had the same roots. We both had strong and sometimes frightening relationships with a parent who demanded too much of us. Cecelia deserved much more credit than my father was giving her. She was fierce in ways I longed to be.

My attitude toward sex changed completely too. For the first time in my life, getting physical felt good. It drove me. Cecelia's body was warm and wet, leaking lavender perfume that left me dizzy when we were done touching each other. Her vulnerability matched my own. Like many teenage girls, she was ashamed of her body and this shattered self-image also fed mine. I knew we had both been wounded, and our hot caresses felt healing—as if with each tentative touch we dissolved our damages. She knew and loved my perverse side. She saw me clearly. I was furious at my father for ridiculing her and trying to ruin our relationship.

I didn't tell anyone in my Jewish clan the truth about my Irish Catholic lover. So far, my parents only suspected we were more than just friends. I didn't want my father to disturb things even more with his provocative comments and criticism. Besides, our clandestine courtship turned me on. I cast my homework aside and secretly called her.

"It's me, hot stuff," I breathed.

"I miss your touch. If you had fingered me for like five more minutes I totally would have blown up and had an orgasm," she confided.

"I'll admit I'm into whatever you want—bondage, role play, public stuff, threesomes. Shit, you could dress me up as a woman and pretend to rape me," I whispered.

"I love you," she giggled.

"I love you too, baby doll," I said.

Cecelia and I made out on street corners, and sometimes she jerked me off in my jeans, or I slipped my hands up under her hot pink skirts. We discovered each other's bodies on the Broadway sidewalk outside Tower Records while people hurried by. This level of exhibitionism let loose something wild in me.

"I wanted to lose my virginity to someone special, and maybe I've found him," Cecelia said one day, kissing me.

"Should we do it at my house or yours?" I asked.

"Let's do it at yours. If my mom caught us, she'd kill us both," Cecelia cooed, rubbing her body against mine.

"I'll make a mix tape of all your favorite songs," I promised.

I waited for a rare night when Mom went to the Synagogue Sisterhood meeting and Dad was going to take Yuvi to see *CATS*.

"Stay home, walk the dog, and don't have any friends over," my father admonished before they left. "Especially Cecelia."

"Here's five dollars for pizza," Mom said as she kissed my cheek and rushed out the door.

As soon as they were gone I ran to my room to light incense and candles and put on the tape I had made for the night with Portishead's low, crooning vocals. I sprayed on some of the Gap's "Blue" cologne that Cecelia had gotten me for Valentine's Day and slipped on the yellow Old Navy boxers that had also been in the gift-wrapped package filled with rose petals. My hands were shaking by the time Cecelia rang our doorbell.

"Did you bring it?" I asked, as I hugged her.

"You smell nice," she said, and smiled, pulling a Lifestyles condom from her purse.

In my room we undressed in the dark, the red numbers on my analog alarm clock blinking at us. I feared sex for the first time would hurt Cecelia too much for her to enjoy it, like I'd read in my body book. She whimpered, then moaned underneath me as I bit and licked her nipples. I felt her body giving before my erection, then a wet rush that held me. The pulsing percussion of Bjork matched my pounding. I glanced at the clock, trying to last, to stretch the time, forever. I came, collapsing onto the narrow bed beside her. When I turned on my light to peel off the condom, it was bloody and she was crying.

"What's the matter? Did I hurt you?" I rubbed her stomach.

"No, I'm just happy it was you," she said.

The next night my parents and Yuvi were sitting down to family dinner when the phone rang.

"We don't pick up when we're eating," Dad said, as he tucked more Italian lemon chicken into his mouth.

"What if it's important?" Mom asked.

"So let them leave a message. I slaved two hours over a hot stove for this meal," my father said.

"Hello?" Mom answered. "It's Cecelia. She sounds very upset," she said and handed me the phone, a concerned frown on her face.

"Cecelia?" I turned away so my family couldn't see me.

"My mom found our condom wrapper," she sobbed. "I'm calling from a payphone. She kicked me out of the house. I have nowhere to go. She won't let me eat or use their phone or Internet. I stole a quarter from her purse when she wasn't looking and—"

"Slow down, calm down," I said in my best impression of my mom's therapist voice.

"She said she was going to sue you for raping me. I haven't had any food since yesterday. What am I going to do? I need a cigarette." Her voice was frantic in my ear.

My parents had an old rotary dial phone attached to the wall that my father refused to get rid of. I didn't know what to say with my family listening, their forks forgotten on their plates.

"She can't do that. You're her daughter," I said.

"What's going on here?" Dad demanded. "If you're getting high and having sex with Cecelia, it needs to end."

"Is everything okay? Are you two having sex?" Mom asked.

"Leave him alone," Yuvi commanded.

"What am I going to do?" Cecelia bawled in my ear.

"No, but Cecelia's mom won't let her eat," I said to my mother. "Can she come have dinner with us?" I asked my parents, as Cecelia continued to cry.

"I'm putting an end to this drama," Dad said, grabbing the phone from me. "Cecelia, this is Hazak's father. I'm a social worker. Look, I know you're upset, but I deal with cases like this all the time. This might be hard to hear, but it's for the best. You need to call child services."

"Let me talk to her," I said and tried to take the phone back.

"I want you to promise me that when I hang up you will call child services. If you don't, the problems with your mom won't stop, they'll just get worse. Great. Good-bye." My father hung up.

"Why did you tell her to do that?" I asked angrily.

"I always knew she was a crazy girl, nothing but neuroses and bad news. Now we can finish our dinner," Dad explained.

"I need to find her," I said, pushing away my plate.

"Hazak, get back here. You belong at this table," my father shouted after me as I rushed out the door.

I sat on her stoop for two hours, but Cecelia never showed up. I imagined her starving and alone, while Dad stuffed his face in peace. When I finally gave up and got home he was waiting.

"Don't ever walk out of here during family dinner." My father shook a finger at me.

"Why did you screw up Cecelia's family even more?" I demanded.

"From the sound of it they were pretty screwed up already. Besides, you were in over your head, Hazak. You can't run around playing psychologist with these damaged girls. My mom was a nut too. I have a degree in this. I know what I'm doing. Cecelia needs to work things out with that bitch of a mother, so I highly suggest you don't see her for a while."

"You don't know anything," I shouted, slamming the door to my room.

Cecelia and I planned a rendezvous in a hasty and secretive AOL Instant Message session. I snuck out to see her that weekend and we walked silently through the San Gennaro festival that my father shunned for its noise. Red, green, blue, and orange lights were strung from the streetlamps of Little Italy. Music, vendor's voices, the pop of burst balloons, and the shrill ringing of sideshow games sounded through the streets. I pushed past the crowds; the smell of spicy sausages sautéed with peppers and stale beer surrounding me somehow made me feel bolder. I bought Cecelia some Zeppolis, fried balls of dough covered in the fine dust of powdered sugar.

"What happened with your mom?" I worked up the courage to ask.

"I should not have called child services. They are going to investigate my mom's job, then my home. There's a possibility I will get taken away. Besides that, my aunt, who never said a harsh word to me ever, cursed me out on the phone. I don't want to be here. I don't want to live."

"She'll never hurt you again," I tried to hug her.

"She really hates your dad and so do I. I never should have called those people," Cecelia pulled away.

"I'm sorry. I shouldn't have let him talk you into it, but you were freaking out when you called me. I couldn't stop him," I explained as we sat on a stoop. We had strayed from the carnival crowds to the dark cobblestone streets of Tribeca.

"I kissed another boy," she said, lighting a Newport. "An Arab."

Instead of the sweet introduction to the world of sex that I'd imagined it to be, Cecelia's mom accused me of rape, and Dad's anger spiraled into a child services' debacle that left me deservedly loveless.

By sophomore year, my petite blonde English teacher was concerned for my mental welfare after I wrote a short story based on Cecelia about a girl getting raped, then committing suicide on a beach in Aruba. I had to do extra credit to bypass a trip to the faculty psychologist. I would stop at nothing to avoid letting another shrink into my life. I would even allow my social worker father into the sacred sanctum of my school. "I'll bring my dad into class. You can meet him and he can talk about his artwork," I said to my teacher.

"Um, why is his ...?" A girl in my class trailed off as she pointed at Dad's painting.

"Why is there an erection sticking out of his pants?" Dad clarified.

My class burst out laughing. The girl and I both blushed.

"That was his ultimate fantasy," my father explained calmly, fingers tracing a female hand holding a gun pointed at the subject's head. "He wanted to be shot in the face by a beautiful woman at the height of sexual stimulation."

"Your dad is so cool," my classmate Dave said afterwards. My friends crowded around me in the hall. It was the first time my father had made me more popular by proxy. His colorful shirts, paint-splattered pants, and scraggly grey beard would come to be sought-after accessories to my artsy classmates.

"He's inappropriate," I told them, walking away. I felt like Dad had just sent me a mental message, in front of my entire English class, warning me his dick would always be bigger.

After that disaster, I hated the routine of school. I started wearing the same dark green hooded sweatshirt everyday, pulling it over my head whenever I passed Cecelia in the hallways. When I got home, I went right to my room and fell asleep, lying to my parents about doing homework and studying for tests. I started hanging out with downtown friends who smoked pot and drank, who laughed about their acid trips, and who danced confidently down the wide hallways of their parent's lofts.

We were obsessed with David Bowie and Andy Warhol, and with the cold, calculated glamour of a lost downtown New York our parents had been on the fringes of. Stealing from their liquor cabinets and blowing pot smoke heavy with secrecy from cracked windows into warm city nights, it seemed I could become someone bolder and brighter: a shiny-lipped youth proudly pouting in the flashes from our Polaroid cameras. I stopped eating, punishing the pounds on my stomach that my father had so loved to pinch. It seemed in leanness there was a power. I wore tight jeans and pointed boots and had my hair cut on a friend's fire escape into Bowie's shaggy mullet. I tried cocaine. Cigarettes began replacing the gum I had once consumed for Dad's decoration. Still, my mouth was a starving one. There was a hunger in me that never went away.

When school started again in September, I was sitting in first period on the top floor of LaGuardia in one of the coveted painting studios that had huge floor-to-ceiling windows looking out over the city and the Hudson River. The sky was bright and blue and I was daydreaming rather than working on my canvas. The head of the art department, a short woman with wiry grey hair, came in and called my teacher aside as I looked on wondering. My teacher gasped and clasped her hands over her mouth, her eyes wide with disbelief.

"Everyone pack up your brushes, cover your canvases, and go on to your next class immediately," my teacher called as disgruntled students groaned and tried to put finishing touches on their flattering self-portraits.

My next period, at 9:30 a.m., was honors English with Mr. Roth, a teacher who had been accused of molesting a female student. He was always late and dressed completely in black the whole time we studied Hamlet. As he rushed in, the class buzzed with excitement and curiosity. The sudden schedule change meant something big was happening. But trapped in the confines of the school walls, we weren't sure what.

"We are under attack," Mr. Roth stated bluntly when he swept into the room in his usual black attire, his blue eyes popping out from his pudgy face. "The World Trade Center has been bombed."

I sat stunned as the class burst into startled cries. I thought this must be another one of his strange teaching methods, but as kids started turning on their cell phones and tried reaching frantic relatives through the crackling static, the news sunk in. I quickly drew a mental map of my family's whereabouts. Yuvi would be far from Tribeca, at middle school in Chelsea, where I had gone. Dad was safe in his studio; Mom was working at St. Vincent's Hospital, now caught in a sudden stream of wounded, but herself unharmed (though I wouldn't know that for sure until later). Mr. Roth turned on a radio, then called out like a sportscaster, "Another body has hit the ground! Fire! People are jumping left and right." He made thudding noises as the class burst into chaos. Outside I could hear stampeding in the halls.

Finally, the class was called to order by our principal's voice crackling over the loudspeaker system: "No one will be allowed to leave the building until picked up by a parent or guardian. Please stay calm and remain in your classroom until a student representative comes to collect you."

I felt strangely removed from my crying classmates, as if none of this was really happening. Mr. Roth read Hamlet's famous soliloquy, "To be, or not to be . . . that is the question." This was his big moment, and he relished being in the spotlight. The drama majors also snatched the opportunity to perform, shrieking and sobbing. Some even hyperventilated, shoving others down onto the floor. Fame had always been a refuge to me, something comforting I could dream of when reality was too harsh to face. Now I saw the dark side of it, how hungry fame monsters used tragedy as an opportunity to take center stage.

✳

"I'm so glad you're here," I cried, when Dad came to pick me up on his bike. I rushed to hug him.

"Me too," he said. "The subways are down, so we'll have to walk home. Your brother and mom will meet us there."

Through the crowds of kids, I saw Cecelia, her face streaked with tears.

"Hold on," I told Dad, pushing my way over to her.

"Hey," she hiccupped.

"Are you okay? Is your family?" I asked.

"Yeah, they're fine. I'm waiting for my mom to come get me," she answered.

"After this is all over, let's be friends," I said, hugging her.

Then I reunited with Dad.

I felt like my father was my hero as we began the miles-long walk downtown. His tampering with Cecelia, sex, child services, even my desire for fame faded and was forgiven as I clung to his side. In the suddenly strange and frightening city, he had come through and was protecting me. We didn't see any people on empty Tenth Avenue, but passing 42nd Street and 34th Street, mad crowds rushed through a sea of honking traffic, disregarding stop signs and oncoming cars, screaming on their cell phones or collapsing on corners and weeping. It felt like a giant film set for a movie about the end of the world.

"I was working in my studio at home, when I heard an explosion. I ran outside just in time to see the second plane hit from our stoop," Dad said, and I squeezed his hand. We stumbled in silence through Union Square. The air started to smell acrid and sweet. Ash and burnt papers blew past us. We stopped in a shabby Chinese take-out restaurant handing out bottles of water to sweaty people fleeing from downtown Manhattan. As I scarfed chicken lo mein my father bought for me and we walked against the tide of survivors, I realized I hadn't eaten since I woke up at 6:30 a.m.

By the time we got through the police barricades at Houston Street to our building I imagined the scent rising above the usual New York pollution was burning flesh. The Lower East Side was about a mile from the towers. Unlike the streets of my school uptown, the streets of my neighborhood were completely deserted and the air of disaster impossibly thicker. When we got to our door and saw smoke streaming endlessly into the sky, Dad suddenly hugged me tight and said, "Thank God you're safe."

That night, my brother and I sat in silence as we watched footage of planes crashing into the towers on the TV he had finally saved up for. As the screen filled with static, I shuddered. Crisis made life clearer, stripped away longings and made small comforts profound: water splashing as my mother brushed her teeth, Dad's padded feet pacing the halls, the warm yellow color of my little brother's bedroom walls. These, not stardom, were the signs I should hope for.

Soon, Osama bin Laden would have the most famous face in the world.

Part II

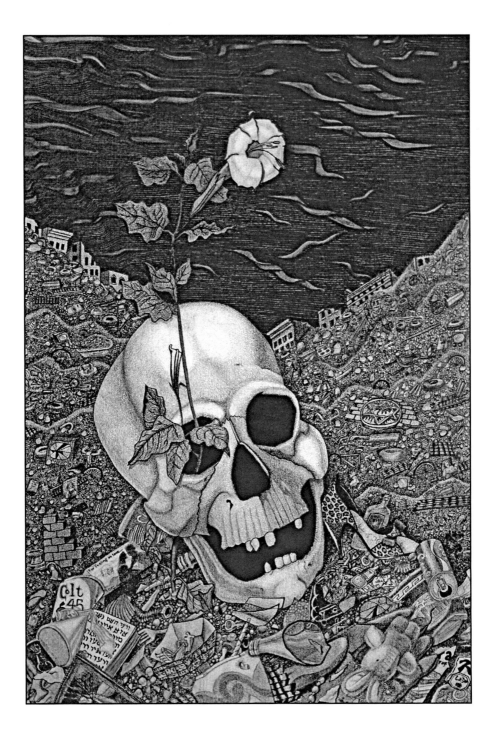

8
Clothing Optional

My departure from the bustling streets of New York had an air of grandeur, as Dad chauffeured eighteen-year-old me into the land of snowy mountains and maple syrup. Mom sat in the front seat of our rental car with a map, while Yuvi took pictures of his new Nikes with Dad's digital camera.

"I know you're having some separation anxiety," my father said, looking at me in the rearview mirror.

"I keep telling you I'm not," I replied.

I was looking forward to what I thought would be a luxurious four years in idyllic nature. I wanted to divorce myself from the city where I had lived with ash, debris, and disaster. Rolling green hills were as far away from 9/11 and its crashed-in cars on Canal Street as I could imagine. Even two years later images of my city in ruin haunted me.

"It's only natural that you should feel some anxiety," Dad said. "Don't worry. We can call and e-mail, and parents' weekend will be here before you know it," he added as he nervously drove the Toyota—packed with my Smiths' poster and my stereo—up Bennington College's winding drive.

"Relax, Dad," I advised.

"We're just concerned. This is a big leap. You've never lived outside the city," Mom explained.

"The city feels empty," I replied.

"Look at all these trees. It's a nice place to visit but I wouldn't want to live here," Dad said. "But it seems like a great school. See, despite all that whining about not being able to spend your Hanukah money, your smart parents' idea for a college fund has paid off."

Bennington had a law that you could go to class naked, as long as you brought a towel to sit on. It had a history of "Dressed to Get Fucked" parties, drinking, and cocaine overdoses. What interested me more were its famous literary alums like Bret Easton Ellis and Jonathan Lethem. I'd read and loved *American Psycho* and *Gun, with Occasional Music.* Since my childhood bedtime story sessions with Dad—his tenor voice carefully rounding out the words of Dostoevsky, Dickens, and Somerset Maugham's *Of Human Bondage* so that they took meaning in my young mind—writing had always been a part of my life. But like most things I held the closest, becoming a writer seemed like an ambition too fantastic, too generous for the world to allow me.

My parents and Yuvi helped me carry my bags into a small white-walled dorm room with someone else's computer and button-up, short-sleeve plaid shirts already strewn on one of two narrow beds.

"It's so lame you still don't own a TV," Yuvi commiserated, looking around.

"I guess we should leave," Dad said.

I turned to see my roommate, Alex Stein from Pasadena, who I had been exchanging e-mails with all summer, paused awkwardly in the doorframe. He wore thick-rimmed glasses and had wild curly brown hair dripping wet from the shower. He was naked, blushing, and still wrapped in a flimsy towel, a puddle forming under his toes.

"Nice to meet you," Mom said and burst out laughing.

"They're leaving soon," I glowered, embarrassed.

When we got outside the four of us stood in front of the Toyota. I didn't know what to say, so I stuffed my hands deep in the pockets of my green hoodie.

"Living without us is going to be really difficult at first," Dad said.

"But before you know it, you'll be home for Thanksgiving and hot home-cooked meals," Mom added, and started to cry.

"Oh, stop it," my father reprimanded.

"Yeah mom, you still have me," Yuvi said.

"Sorry, I can't help it." Mom wiped away her tears.

"I love you," I said, hugging each of my family in turn.

"We love you too, sweetie," Dad said.

"I'll miss you." Yuvi patted me on the back.

"One more, for good luck," Mom said, squeezing me hard again and pressing her face against my chest.

"I want a good-bye shot," my father announced as he grabbed his digital camera back from Yuvi. I looked off at the endless gray sky, oddly void of tall buildings. The camera clicked and a flash momentarily blinded me, the light hanging in the air as my family pulled away.

"Want to invite the girls who live in the room next door to William-stown?" Alex Stein asked. "I hear they have a Thai restaurant."

"Definitely."

After just an hour, I already felt like I had to get off the campus and its surrounding woods. It reminded me of Maine's menacing wilder-ness—a lonely place it seemed too easy to get lost in.

"I better get into film history class," I said as we drove past stands selling pumpkins off the highway. As the wind whipped back my hair I felt a rush of freedom. My parents had urged me to study psycholo-gy. Mom claimed I was "astute and understanding," but I guessed she really hoped I would one day get a degree like her. Bennington had no requirements and no grades, a place where I could escape my parents' suffocating expectations. I didn't want to overanalyze all the smallest interactions. College was going to be a fun, free place where I could let go.

One of our female neighbors had brought a dark-haired boy named Casey along for the ride, and he shared my enthusiasm.

"Dude, I totally want to take that class, too," Casey said, giving me a high five. As we walked down the desolate Main Street, our neighbor talked about Casey a mile a minute, already dishing dirt though we had just met.

"The only reason I made out with him is because his dad is Bruce Willis's lawyer. They live in 90210," She admitted.

I glanced at Casey, trailing behind us, looking self-conscious in mismatched designer clothes. It seemed that every time fame faded from my mind a sacred sign showed up, shining as I imagined the Hollywood sign did at night. I wanted to meet Bruce Willis.

When we got back to campus later, I felt more claustrophobic than before, surrounded by countryside.

"I need concrete," I sighed, throwing myself on my bed.

As I stared at the walls, wondering where I should hang the postcard of a painting my dad had made, which he had given me as a parting gift—women with red afros doing the can-can in a chorus line—the phone rang. I picked it up eagerly. "Hello?"

"Hi, sweetie, how are you settling in?" Mom sounded nervous and upset.

"All the food around here sucks, and there are way too many fat white people. What's wrong?" I asked.

"We got lost on the way home. You know how these crowded highways are. I hate cars." She dodged my question.

"Hello? Hazak?" Dad picked up the other line.

"What's going on?" I asked.

"You didn't tell him?" Dad sounded annoyed.

"I thought—" Mom paused.

"Nancy has uterine cancer," my father stated bluntly.

I hadn't seen Fancy Nancy since she moved to Mexico four years before, ending our annual holiday shopping sprees and nights watching movies and talking at her Upper West Side home. I still e-mailed her long distance, craving her tales of saving stray dogs in San Miguel de Allende and looking to her for answers to my angsty teenage problems.

"Are you okay?" Mom asked.

"I'm fine," I said, clenching my teeth so I wouldn't cry in front of Alex, who was staring at me over the edge of his Mac laptop.

"She's tough. She'll pull through," Dad said. "The important thing is that you're doing okay without your father and mother."

"I need to go, love you both," I said and hung up halfway through the sound of Mom making kissing noises.

"It's our first night here. Let's get drunk," I said to Alex, who had smuggled some weed and a jug of Carlo Rossi Merlot onto campus. Soon I had ripped off my shirt and we were head banging to Siouxsie and the Banshees, screaming lyrics at the top of our lungs. There was a timid knock on the door and when I opened, Casey stood there, nervously staring at me.

"What's up dudes?" Casey looked down at my bare ribs.

"Join the party," I slurred, dragging him into the room.

Casey perched awkwardly on my bed, shooting nervous glances at me while I thrashed to the blasting music and chugged wine from the jug.

"Burn me," I demanded, shoving my lit Marlboro Red at Casey. "Draw swastikas on my arm, like Siouxsie at her shows."

"But I'm Jewish," he protested.

"So am I, asshole," I garbled.

I wanted to impress him, forget the bad news my parents had delivered over miles of telephone wire. I felt like the only way to stick out in the midst of creative kids who wore flip flops and tie-dyed ponchos was to be as tough and outrageously New York as possible. I tried to smolder, like the city I had left behind. I guided his fingers down and felt the cigarette butt burn my flesh.

%&$#?@!

As I was registering for film history class in a big remodeled barn the next day an older boy with small, pursed lips (which I found instantly repugnant), a lopsided, spectacled fleshy face, and a rakish Burberry hat came up to me in line.

"I'm Evelyn," he said and held out his hand.

"Hazak," I muttered.

His palm was clammy when we touched.

"Back home in Kentucky you'd get lynched with a kike name like that," he drawled, smiling at me.

"I'm from New York," I said and turned away.

"Hey, I was just joking. You have beautiful blue eyes." He still hovered at my shoulder.

"They're gray and I'm not into guys. Why don't you go away?" I suggested.

"Everyone ends up screwing everything here," he announced.

"I'm not interested," I said.

"I was kicked out of my old college for fucking a professor. We spent a year traveling abroad until he dumped me, so I got wasted and took on a group of Marines bareback," Evelyn murmured near my ear, before moving away. His breath smelled like gin and Camembert cheese.

I later learned there were all sorts of fantastic rumors about Evelyn floating around campus. He seemed to enjoy the talk, even when it turned ugly. Snatches of gossip reached my ears at "Thirsty Thursdays," tequila-infused parties in crammed dorm rooms.

"I heard he was named after his great-uncle Evelyn Waugh. He's so *Brideshead Revisited.*"

"I heard his grandfather comes from old Southern money and was one of the founders of the KKK."

"I heard his mom and dad molested him."

Parties quickly became the chaotic backdrops against which I played out my self-destruction. I discovered I could drink long and hard, that this was expected and admired from a tall boy in his freshman year at a school where there was nothing better to do. Liquor was my course of study. In the blackest of moments, I replaced the feeling that fame had given me, that power I had chased my whole life, with oblivion.

Nothing mattered and I was the king of reckless abandon. Campus security quickly caught on and spotted me as a troublemaker before I even knew it myself. They began trailing me back to my dorm from classes, quickly shining their flashlights in my eyes as we passed on the dark Bennington roads. Their glinting badges, and the glowing eyes of small creatures in the dark trees, haunted my drunken sprees, but also heightened their drama. I felt constantly hunted. One night, running from Security after a particularly raucous house party where I had run through the house hitting people in the face—I was too drunk to land anything but ineffectual slaps—while calling them "cunts," I bumped into Casey. He was standing in the middle of one of the lanes of houses, looking like he was about to cry.

"Are you okay?" I asked.

"Hey," he grabbed my arm and held tight. "Can you take a walk with me?"

"Sure." I wondered if he was feeling as lonely as I was in this tiny, alcohol-fueled village of academia. I imagined his hometown of L.A. was an even more hectic and star-studded city than New York. We walked out onto the End of the World, Bennington's infamous expanse of lawn, stretching shadowy and seemingly endlessly in the middle of campus, which was stopped by a wall of short stones visible only in the sun.

"Some guy stuck his hand down my pants at the party," Casey blurted.

"He was probably just drunk."

"I know. I'm not mad, just afraid people are going to think I'm a fag."

"If he came up to you and shoved his hand down your pants I don't see how that makes you gay. Some senior guy named Evelyn tried to hit on me; it's not a big deal. Everyone screws everything here."

"Two years ago Evelyn was driving wasted and went straight off a cliff," Casey said, suddenly perking up, "It was a miracle he survived. He told everyone it was an accident and since he tipped the nurses so well, they left him alone."

"How do you know that?" I asked.

"Oh someone told me," he muttered. "Anyway, I'm afraid that asshole queer molesting me might leak on Page Six. My dad is in there all the time."

The next day Casey started sitting next to me in our film history class, in the campus movie theater. Our teacher Steven was a lean ex-Hollywood producer who chain-smoked Marlboro Lights at breaks and screened early silent films like *The Great Train Robbery*. His lectures were peppered with juicy gossip about the stars. Clark Gable was a gigolo for male and female Hollywood royalty before his big break. Every major film star had been an alcoholic. Steven had once lunched with Vivien Leigh after she'd starred in *Gone with the Wind*.

"She was a beautiful psychotic," he rasped as I sat taking eager notes. Screen legends and their debauched lives fueled my fantasies.

Charlie Chaplin, Clark Gable, Marlon Brando played in my mind endlessly, when I wasn't in film class soaking in their fame.

I loved sitting in the dark movie theater, lost in black and white worlds that weren't mine. As we watched Chaplin's *City Lights* I was reminded of the Olive Tree Café on MacDougal Street, where my mother, and then later Nancy, used to take my brother and me for dinners, where we gorged on falafels smothered in hummus. The restaurant screened Charlie Chaplin movies and had chalkboard tables you could draw on. As the story of a tramp masquerading as a millionaire to win the love of a blind flower girl ended, I cried silently. My classmates burst into disrespectful laughter.

"Loser!" One shouted at the screen.

"I hate these elitist hippies," I fumed as I stormed out the nearest exit, Casey running to catch up.

"They're not like us, dude. We're going to leave here and I'll make you famous in L.A.," he panted, as I lit a Marlboro Red.

"For a bunch of Dead Heads that claim to love everything, they really make me feel like shit. How could anyone laugh at that kind of loneliness?" I asked.

"The last time I saw Bruce Willis, he said I was handsome," Casey said, grinning. "Cheer up. Over the summer we'll stay at my family's mansion in Beverly Hills."

Casey knew, understood, and played to the part of me that lusted for the spotlight, the glow of fame framing my figure and transforming personal tragedy into universal art. Yet I was more like Chaplin's tramp than I cared to admit: desperate to impress, clumsily alone. After films, Casey filled me in on his days as a sixth-grade meth head and all the surfer girls he had slept with back west. He made electronic music and invited me to his room to play songs for me.

"So you grew up on the Lower East Side? My dad used to live in the Bronx. He said the subway windows had bullet holes in them," Casey shared.

"Yeah, my dad moved to Crosby Street in the '60s. The mob used to dump dead bodies on his block," I told him.

"My mom grew up in Great Neck, out in Long Island. Have you ever been there?" Casey asked.

"Are you serious? My mom grew up there too. They probably went to the same high school. My Babbi and Zayde still live there." I was thrilled by this connection.

"You're like my East Coast counterpart," Casey grinned.

I smiled, wishing it were true.

I started writing e-mails to Yuvi in New York. With Nancy sick, I suddenly realized what an important past he and I shared. I also wanted to help him get through his first real-life taste of death. He wrote me an e-mail:

"DEAR HAZAK,

SINCE YOU LEFT EVERYTHING KIND OF HIT ME. I DON'T KNOW WHAT TO FEEL, EXCEPT FOR LOST. I THINK ABOUT LIFE AND HOW FUCKING STUPID IT IS AND HOW ANNOYING IT IS—ALL THE PHILOSOPHICAL STUPID BULLSHIT THAT MAKES ME FEEL SOOOOO EMPTY. BUT THAT DOESN'T MATTER BECAUSE I FEEL LIKE THE ONLY PERSON WHO I CAN RELATE TO IN ANY WAY IS YOU."

I needed to be there for Yuvi and Nancy, not trapped in a prison of spiteful limousine liberals in the middle of nowhere, earning a degree my parents desperately wanted for me. But without any perspective, my imagination ran wild and I started acting like a celebrity lost in the woods.

Casey decided we should start a band called Partyboy International with me as lead singer.

"I recommend cool new music to this writer at *Rolling Stone*. He'll totally cover us," Casey said, enthusiastically. I pictured Bruce Willis listening to our demo and immediately started writing songs with depressing lyrics.

We were slated to have our debut performance at the campus bar's annual Battle of the Bands.

"We're going to win. You're totally hot, babe," Casey said, grinning and pinching my cheek before the show.

"Sure," I said, blowing cigarette smoke in his face to make him back off and chugging a giant glass of gin and orange juice. I figured in L.A. everyone called each other "babe," but it made me uncomfortable to be so close to him.

By the time I climbed on stage, I was belligerent. The overhead lights glared in my eyes. That, combined with the liquor, made my blood hum, out of control and alive. Everyone was sitting on the floor, lazily nodding their heads and fiddling with their Birkenstock straps.

"I'm not singin' till you motherfuckers get up and dance!" I screamed into the mic. I noticed campus Security in a corner glaring at me, but I didn't care. They could only cite you for open containers and all I had in my hand was a cheat sheet of lyrics I had been too drunk to memorize. The crowd rose and we launched into our set. Our biggest groupie, who had a huge crush on Casey, was a girl named Liz with triple-D tits. She jumped on stage, flailing wildly. As people started to dance and cheer, I felt more ecstatic and aroused than I had all term. Not able to play any musical instruments, my thoroughly modern attitude was that I played my persona instead. Swaggering through a set, I was bolstered by booze. People didn't really like me at Bennington, but everyone knew who I was. A sensation crept through the too-loud music: being a shocking and spectacular vision was easy for me when the stage on which I sang was so small.

%&$#?@!

After the set, Casey and I rushed back to my room for an exclusive after-party, just the two of us. After doing shots of Jim Beam, I collapsed on my bed on the verge of passing out. Casey climbed in and wrapped his arms around me.

"You were great tonight, dude," he whispered, licking my ear. "I remember when I was five, I snuck into my parents' bed after having a nightmare. Just my dad was there and he got a hard on against my back while he was sleeping. I liked it," he murmured as I felt his sudden erection pressing against my spine.

I thought of my own father painting penises in his studio. Finally, I'd met someone even more fucked up by his dad's dick than I was. I turned to face him, so I could get away from his stiffness and analyze the situation.

"What mental implications do you think that experience had?"

"They were all innocuous," Casey whispered, leaning in and licking my lips. "Why can't we do this when you're sober?" he nibbled my ear.

"We can," I lied.

All my rock icons—David Bowie, Mick Jagger, Lou Reed—had slept indiscriminately with both men and women. Here was my chance to experience the strange and different feel of a rougher touch. As always, if someone famous had done it, I wanted to do it too. Evelyn's words hung in my mind. How much more interesting would I be if I could claim a bisexual liaison? *At least try it once,* I thought.

But my body betrayed me. I felt myself shrink instinctively from Casey's touch. His smell—like Play-Doh, his mom's detergent, and the jojoba oil he had told me he masturbated with—lingered on his fingertips and made me nauseous. I was afraid to tell him the truth: I had to be drunk to try to kiss him. Sober, I could only flirt with the idea in my head—a comfortable place where Bowie pranced in a black leather jacket singing "John, I'm Only Dancing." With liquor coursing through me I could disassociate. It was what I had almost always done with sex: part of me shut off, letting my body be touched while my mind went blank. Maybe in my current state I could give Casey what he wanted. I leaned in and kissed him, stubble grating against stubble. He moaned into my mouth. I kept my eyes open and watched his thick, dark eyebrows furrow with desire. My shoulders were rigid, my whole body tensed. I pulled away before I could stop myself.

"I get it. We're just friends," Casey said, getting up, trying to hide his hard-on as he rushed over to my roommate's bed. Alex was spending the night with his girlfriend.

"I need to take a shower," I said, quickly grabbing a towel and leaving the room, heavy relief in each sloppy step I took to create distance between us. With the cool tiles of the bathroom beneath my feet, I scrubbed my hands, and also the places he hadn't touched—my chest, my cock. I let hot water rush into my mouth, scalding away the taste of alcohol and Casey. Drunk and soapy, I accidentally slit my fingers open on my rusty razor blade.

When I got back to the room, my hand wrapped in soaked-through bloody red toilet paper, Casey was grinning up at me from Alex's bed.

"I cut myself," I showed him, as if the wound was proof of my feelings for him. We could be blood brothers, bandmates, best friends. That I would give him gladly.

"I just jerked off, dude," Casey said, ignoring my outstretched hand. "Best orgasm, like, ever."

I crawled into my own bed and as I reached to turn out the lights, Casey lifted his sheets, exposing the spent arch of his erection. It was the last part of him I saw.

%&$#?@!

When I woke up Casey was gone and Alex was playing his guitar. As details from the night before penetrated my foggy head, I noticed the red message light on my phone was blinking.

"Hey dude, it's Casey. There's like this bad cough going around campus and you know I'm really afraid of germs, so I left early. I'm at the airport on my way to L.A. I don't think I'll be coming back. USC has a great film program."

I was confused and devastated, determined I had done something wrong. Casey knew I was straight. Had he flown thousands of miles away because I wouldn't hook up with him? I felt guilty and wished I'd been able to give him what he wanted. Clark Gable had slept his way to the top with men and women. And this was the enlightened post-millennium. No one had sexual hang-ups anymore. No one cared where I put my prick. Except me. I had this haunting, horrible feeling that I only wanted to have sex with girls who I loved. I was more conservative with my body than my peers, my father, the American populace.

Obviously, if I wanted to make it I had to grow up and stop being such a prude. Dad had chosen social work over artistic success. I didn't want to spend four more years getting a safe degree; I wanted full-blown fame, and if that meant using my body as a tool, I decided I would do it.

I couldn't believe I'd lost my bassist, best friend, and Bruce Willis connect with my stupid hesitation. What and who I desired didn't matter—it never really had. Unable to soothe my own loneliness, I should at least have had the balls to ball away his. Shocked and alone, I stumbled, hungover, through knee-high snow to Casey's room, where scattered papers and loose socks were evidence of his hasty departure. I knew he had a handle of Smirnoff vodka under his bed.

"Casey left this for me," I lied to his roommate, grabbing the bottle. It was the only piece left of him. Triple-D Liz seemed the best person to share it with.

In Liz's room we used Stella Artois as a mixer, chugging beer and vodka from giant ceramic mugs.

"Why did Casey leave?" she asked, lighting scented candles.

"I think he's afraid of what I make him feel," I said.

"He's sexy," Liz responded. She poured us more vodka and we grinded to the radio, then collapsed, exhausted, amidst the pink pillows on her bed.

"You know, you kind of look like him," Liz said, and hiccupped.

"Who?" I asked.

"Casey," she said, leaning in and kissing me.

I ripped off her shirt and her massive breasts spilled around my neck, her large pale pink nipples slipping into my mouth. I moaned as she pulled off my pants and I slipped my fingers through her panties and inside her.

"What a cute couple," said Liz's roommate, sarcastically, slamming the door of their room and waking us up. I looked over at Liz, who pulled the covers over her face. We were both naked, but I couldn't remember if we'd even had sex. My head was pierced with pain; cold winter light poured in the windows, and the somber, haunting chorus of "Hurt" came over the radio. Johnny Cash had died just a few months earlier on September 12.

There was an off-campus art opening that night and I found a designated driver. I knew there would be an open bar and I was desperate for escape—drink, escape, drink. If I hadn't found a car, I would have run, jogging down highways until I could dip my lips to the troughs of free booze. I puffed a fat joint on the way and stared out at the highways lined with endless trees and small farm-stands selling pumpkins. I craved the energy of New York. I imagined Casey happily back in L.A., going to celebrity parties, recuperating from the Vermont winter and me, sitting poolside in dark sunglasses.

At the gallery I drank beer and wine, then gin and orange juice, pocketing a Pabst Blue Ribbon for the drive back to campus with a sober older classman behind the wheel. Halfway back, blue and red lights and the wail of a siren pierced the night. We pulled over and an officer IDed the driver, then shone his flashlight in my eyes.

"How old are you, kid?" he demanded.

"Twenty-eight," I answered, thinking this was a reasonable age.

"Step out of the vehicle."

I handed him my student ID, proving I was actually eighteen, as I swayed by the side of the highway.

"Now I know your real age. This your real name?" he asked, squinting at the piece of plastic.

I nodded.

"Don't look real to me. Arab or something?"

"Jew from New York."

"You like PBR?" the cop asked as he hoisted the beer from my inside pocket after patting me down. "You know kid, one day you're drinking and the next day you're Ted Bundy," he went on. "It will look better for you if you take a Breathalyzer test." He tried to force a tube in my face.

"I'm not drunk," I told him.

"You think I'm stupid? You smell like a saloon floor," he said, pushing the tube at me again.

"I won't take the test," I said stubbornly. I had wanted to get out of my head via the freedom I found at the bottom of bottles. Instead, I was on the verge of being arrested for the first time in my life.

"Have it your way," he said, writing out a ticket for $500. "You're going to have to pay or go to jail. We have a zero tolerance law in Vermont. It says anyone underage drinking is a threat. I'm sure you rich kids at that crazy school have mommies and daddies who can afford alcoholic Jew York brats." My red face burned from liquor and his awful words. I just wanted to get out of his squad car and away.

%&$#?@!

When I finally got back to campus, the first thing I needed to do was drink more to forget the whole thing. My friends in the car had also gotten tickets, but they just laughed and tore them up. The cop had been right about them. To their families drinking and hundreds of dollars wasn't a big deal—just some harmless trouble that was par for the course at the old artsy alma mater. My parents had opened an account for me at the Bank of Bennington with five hundred dollars for the entire term. I had spent all of it already and knew they wouldn't help me pay my fine, because I had been drunk. Except for one glass of Manischewitz on Jewish holidays, they almost never touched liquor. Based on their experiences with their clients, they placed drinkers in two categories: completely sober like themselves or hopelessly alcoholic, like Evelyn.

For such a shame, a Jewish *shanda*, I might as well have gotten caught shooting heroin. After chugging a bottle of Gordon's gin I called my parents, wasted and sobbing, huddled on the floor of my dorm's public phone booth. My roommate, Alex, was busy practicing in our room for next day's naked Frisbee tournament.

"Hello?" My father answered, sounding tired.

"It's me. Is Mom there?" I asked. I needed comfort and knew I wouldn't get it from him.

"She's asleep, it's three in the morning. You sound funny, what's going on?"

"I feel so alone here," I blubbered, "So stagnant. I'm supposed to be getting famous and I'm trapped in the middle of nowhere."

"Hazak, have you been drinking?" Dad's voice came clear and sharp.

"My best friend flew back to L.A., and this cop was obviously racist and harassing me. I think he was drunk too," I said.

"Mister, you're drunk and you're not making sense."

"Please don't hang up. I'm so lonely," I said. I saw shadows of feet pass by under the phone booth door and started to shake uncontrollably.

"Where are you?" Dad asked.

"In my dorm, hiding. Everyone knows your business; it's so small here. They say this is the most important year of your life and I'm wasting it in fucking Vermont," I wailed.

"So now you're depressed? Life isn't fair," Dad responded curtly. "When I turned sixty I started feeling depressed. We were on a family vacation in Maine and I asked you if you'd noticed anything different about me and you said no. You hurt my feelings."

I slammed down the receiver, staggered into my room past a startled Alex, and started throwing the countless empty liquor bottles that had been littering my closet out the window. They hurtled through the dead, leafless trees, falling, dark marks against the snow.

9
Southern Comfort

I was preoccupied with Casey's abandonment and had no interest in academics. Bennington felt like a fever dream crusted in ice. Using Casey's lie, I told my parents I was sick and had to come home early, planning to load my bags onto a bus back to New York.

"But don't expect me to help carry any of your stuff," Dad warned.

My real plan was never to return to Vermont.

Later that day, as the bus pulled into Port Authority, the city rushed to remind me of its rhythm, the panicked pace that had ruled my life and that my bones now fell back into effortlessly. Everything made me smile: crackheads with darting eyes dodging under subway turnstiles, the smell of fried doughnuts, spilled beer. Ads illuminated, taxis honking, buildings soaring—all momentarily startled me after the quiet of the country. How loudly everything screamed: lives are made here! And mine would be too.

Yet when I got off the train in the Lower East Side, lugging garbage bags of clothes down the street—I loved that no one stopped to offer me help—the surroundings of my childhood had completely changed. In the few short months I had been at Bennington, bistros and candlelit wine bars had replaced corner bodegas. I felt disoriented, looking for the lost landmarks of my youth. It was an early summer night and in the growing dark, high heels clicked past sidewalk tables, white napkins were pressed to lips, laughter and perfume lingered on corners. No open hydrants gurgled, no clacking Domino games sounded on milk-crate tables, no sweet weed floated from windows with its promise of transforming reality into something kinder. I had come home to a place I no longer knew.

My parents, too, seemed excited, but more distant. Dinner was laid out, but the discussion was all about when I would return to school. I swallowed numbly, not even taking in the conversation or concerned looks that Mom and Dad passed each other along with their plates. That night, my lie turned true as I lay in bed and was suddenly sweat-sticky with fever. My city, my family, myself were distorted beyond recognition with flu.

%&$#?@!

When I got better, instead of telling my parent's my true plans, I started going to visit Evelyn at his Brooklyn loft. Though Evelyn shared stories of his unprotected orgies with sailors during Fleet Week at his loft in Carroll Gardens, he also had sleek designer furniture and stacks of first edition T. S. Eliot collections and literary quarterlies I'd never heard of. Scraps of notebook paper covered in his minute scrawling hand held the poetry he never shared with me. It made sense that real geniuses never read their work aloud to kids like me. I imagined his prolific prose works were glorious and was sure some of his literary talent would leak into me with the drinks he poured us. Empty bottles of Veuve Clicquot lined his windowsills.

"When did you drink all this champagne?" I asked.

"I drink more than that queer bastard Capote," he laughed. "And hopefully I'll die younger."

I sipped Veuve with him while watching "Party Monster," the shockumentary about Michael Alig, a junkie party promoter who infamously murdered his drug dealer.

"What a trashy freak," Evelyn exclaimed after the film, his high-pitched Southern chuckle ringing through the apartment. "I'm going to get my loaded degenerate daddy to give me Warhol's *Campbell's Soup Can* print so I can hang it over my stairway."

"I wish my father made art as good as Warhol," I said.

"He made you," Evelyn winked.

The next night, he showed me old pictures of himself and the professor who had fucked him—Evelyn looked young, handsome, and happy. I wondered how it was humanly possible to drink so much that he was bloated at age twenty-four. Was he on antidepressants? Was it because of the car accident? He had a passion for rich food, creamy cheeses, baguettes, and foie gras, which he crammed down his throat with liquor.

After showing me his flashback photographs, Evelyn took me to a private party at the new Limelight, proudly displaying me on his arm, so I could see where Alig used to promote every night.

"You know I fucked Rufus Wainwright once while we listened to these albums," Evelyn told me when we were back in Brooklyn later that night. His eyes turned melancholy while he chugged gin and sang along to Billie Holiday.

"I don't care. Just give me another drink," I demanded.

"You look hotter when you're mean," he said, pouring.

Every night for the next week we went to bars where he was chummy with the bartender. I didn't mind when, wasted, he'd insist on hand-feeding me bar nuts as long as I was drinking too. I was broke and he was loaded; he always picked up the tab with a condescending air. We were both posturing—he was desperately lonely and I was addicted to the lush life and his audience-like attention.

I was the only person Evelyn knew in New York that he hadn't estranged with his excessive drinking and condescension. The more I saw of him, the more I realized I embodied everything he had lost: youth, looks, drive. I feared I could end just as used up as he.

Evelyn invited me to gay Indie filmmaker John Cameron Mitchell's birthday party at Happy Ending, a remodeled Chinese brothel around the corner from my parents' house, and I eagerly rushed over in my tightest white jeans.

"Where are you going dressed like that?" my father wanted to know.

"Honestly, Hazak, you look so silly," Mom said, laughing.

"I'm going down the block to John Cameron Mitchell's birthday party," I announced.

"Isn't he the guy who did *Hedwig and the Angry Inch*? That was a really fantastic, artsy play," Dad responded. He seemed thrilled. No matter how much my parents distrusted my penchant for following fame, they were still strangely impressed when I dropped certain names. I would learn everyone was.

"Be home by eleven," Mom called as I ran down the stairs.

I knew the crowd would all be gay, but I didn't care. I rationalized I was comfortable enough with my masculinity to play with it. Hadn't my own father plumbed the perverse depths of the human psyche with his provocative artwork? As long as it didn't go further, I thought I could handle flirting in a bid for fame. I knew with my provocative pants, bulge, and blue-eyed, smooth-shaved face, I could charm the crowd. I perceived this as my power, not realizing my outfit and careless attitude was really armor against crippling loneliness. I was desperation dressed in the drag of a downtown hustler.

"The doorman didn't card you because he said no one under twenty-one would dress like a gigolo," Evelyn smirked.

I laughed him off, like I was the life of the party. I made friends with a pretty girl who I tried to seduce by asking her to put lipstick on me.

"Oh my god! Alan Cumming!" She shrieked halfway through, pointing behind my shoulder and smearing red down my cheek. With real celebs around no one cared about a no-name like me, and I was pushed and shoved out of the way by fawning fans.

By the time trannies were dishing dirt for the birthday roast on a makeshift stage covered in glitter, I was wasted and slumped sullenly in a corner of the club with a mute midget who kept climbing on the bar and writing his drink orders on napkins. I commiserated with him—we were the outcasts of the party. To the country-bred kids on my insular Vermont campus, I was the cool boy from New York City. But back in the city I was just another throwaway hopeful on a cutthroat island.

"My friend likes you," Evelyn slurred as he sidled over to me.

"I told you. I'm not into men," I said, brushing him off.

"He could make you famous," Evelyn grinned.

I followed his finger to a tall, pasty-looking guy with puffy red-rimmed eyes. He looked like my father, balding and scruffy.

"What does he do?" I asked.

"He works for John," Evelyn replied mysteriously, nudging me. "I bet he could get you a job."

"Whatever," I groaned, rolling my eyes and clinking drinks with the inebriated midget. But I stored the information away as I chugged.

Later, blacking in and out of consciousness, I let the tall, pasty guy put his tongue in my mouth in an alley, with my eyes open, staring over his shoulder. His stubble scratching my face reminded me of my father's beard, and I had to fight to keep from throwing up. As I stumbled home I pissed myself, yellow trailing down my white jeans. Mom woke me up the next day with Evelyn on the phone.

"Sweetie," she said. "There's a man who says he knows you from Bennington. He sounds drunk." She looked concerned.

"Oh, it's just his drawl. He's from Kentucky," I answered, grabbing the cordless. I rolled my eyes at my clock—11:30 a.m. and Evelyn was already hammered.

"Congratulations, you slick eighteen-year-old son of a bitch. You've officially landed an extra role in *Shortbus*, the new John Cameron Mitchell flick."

"I told you not to call me when you're wasted," I said, elated I had gotten a part but ashamed Mom had gotten a hint of my hidden life.

%&$#?@!

When I showed up at an "extras holding" in DUMBO, Brooklyn I was horrified to realize the guy I'd made out with for the extra role was a caterer. I had thought he was at least an assistant cameraman. A lifetime supply of free stale donuts was not worth swapping spit with a dude. I angrily ignored him the whole shoot, sipping moodily on the flask of Jim Beam whisky I had brought for company. I was plain and unsensational compared to the people assembled for filming. They were taller and skinnier, caked with flamboyant makeup, dressed in blazing colors and glittering with costume jewelry.

I trooped over to the elaborate burlesque nightclub set where we were shooting a crowd scene. John Cameron Mitchell gave directions, shouting over a megaphone. For the next three hours I had to hold an empty beer bottle and cheer enthusiastically with the eclectic crowd while Justin Vivian Bond belted out a song from his perch on the bar. I started to resent the roaring crowd, the painted faces drawn in mock hilarity while hungry eyes searched out the camera lens. The room stank of sweat and makeup; women flashed their tits; and Justin pulled down the pants of a dreadlocked young man, laughing high and loud as the man's dark penis was exposed. This impersonal raunchiness disgusted me. I wanted more than this. More real fame. More real love.

While I was smoking a Marlboro Red and leaning against a wall between takes, a gaunt, gaudy gay extra and a plump, scantily clad female friend approached me.

"Hey, stud, you look like a real hooker with that cig. You think my friend Dirty Martini and I can split you after the shoot?" he lisped.

"I'm not for sale," I said with a glare.

Feeling stained and gypped out of a starring role, I finished my whiskey and fled the DUMBO set, taking the train back to Manhattan.

"Did you get paid?" my father asked, when I got home.

"No," I shouted, rushing past him. I slammed the door to my room and sprawled on my bed.

"You can't just leave school and run around doing movie shoots not making any money," Dad called from the other room.

I put on an Ella Fitzgerald CD that Evelyn had lent me and took a handle of Jim Beam from behind my pillow, where I kept my stash. I swallowed my Jimmy with the pleasant sense that I was getting what I wanted.

After Evelyn found out I had exchanged a kiss for a movie role he lashed out at me. He invited me over, then wouldn't serve me a drink, going on a long, wasted rant.

"You good-looking, young, hetero pricks think you can get famous while you're still alive. You want to be a big shot writer with tons of money, fancy cars, mansions, and women. That isn't poetry. I'll drink and suck dick until I die—then they'll discover me. They'll leave flowers on my grave. You'll be a cheap male model or an escort. I haven't had dinner yet. Why don't you let me go down on you?"

"Fuck no, that's gross," I said. I tried to ignore him, thinking this was just the way people made it. My parents had never met Evelyn and didn't know what I was up to; they thought trying to have a career as a famous anything was a waste.

Next time we met, when Evelyn was very drunk, he tried to kiss me and I shoved him back. He tripped over his own wasted limbs, sprawling, his head hitting the floor with a thick crack. I wasn't going to make the same mistake of whoring myself out without a big payoff. Evelyn's eyes were scared and startled, his mouth puckering pathetically as he crawled over to where I still stood in shock. He grabbed at my knees and thighs, trying to hug and hold me.

"I need to be alone to write," he whimpered, "but if I'm alone I drink and then I can't write."

"You can't kiss me," I said. "I'm not gay like you."

"But you kissed the guy at John's party," he argued.

"That was only so I could be in a movie," I replied coldly.

Our friendship was a drunken train wreck—we both lost track of time and conversations, our initial amity drowned in booze. Mirroring the relationship I had with my father, Evelyn's and my ambitions clashed and became a cruel competition.

The next time I came over to his house, he didn't answer the doorbell. I had been counting on him to feed me and I stood among the vines of his Carroll Gardens courtyard, starving, and furious. But as always with Evelyn, my anger gave way to worry and I went to a phone booth around the corner after convincing a guy at a Bodega counter to change my last dollar into quarters. On the final quarter, Evelyn picked up.

"There will be time, there will be time, to prepare a face to meet the faces that you meet." His slow voice was even slower than its usual boozy slur.

"Where the fuck are you?" I shouted. "I've been ringing your doorbell forever."

Evelyn started to laugh. "So you do care, pretty boy," he said. He couldn't stop laughing. "You do care about old me after all."

"What happened to you?" I demanded.

"Oh, I just dove down the stairs," he sighed.

"I'll be right over. I'm around the corner." My fingers were shaking around the shiny black curve of the pay phone handle. I was thinking of his suicide attempts, and his one great, long, and drawn-out daily suicide by sweet liquor. And me, his only handle on the outside world, with my impetuous face, my manipulative smile. A silly young caretaker who, at eighteen, could barely care for himself.

"Go home. You have one," Evelyn said and hung up.

%&$#?@!

After a two-week absence, Evelyn returned from a grand European tour and invited me over to drink absinthe-and-champagne cocktails.

"Hemingway's drink," he said on the phone.

When I got there he showed me photos of ruined castles and reminisced about his attempts to seduce a Welsh priest.

"We had pints every afternoon at this old pub on the edge of town with green hills stretching around us. He was so hot in his habit."

I was wearing cutoff jeans shorts and I got nervous when he glanced at my knees while he talked. Suddenly he put down his drink and grabbed my crotch. I pushed him off, but it only made him more aggressive.

"Come on. I'm hungry," he whined as I shoved his hands away.

"Stop!" I yelled.

He crammed his fingers in and over my mouth. After a few minutes of struggle, I let him pull my shorts down around my ankles. This is what he had always wanted. My body was what I owed him. I watched, pretending I was in a stranger's skin.

"Relax, let me suck your big cock," he murmured.

He took my softness in his hands and didn't stop sucking until I got hard. At least he thought I had a large dick, and I was sure he'd seen a lot of them. My belly and pubic hair were reflected in the hungry gleam of his reading glasses, my penis disappearing between his pouty little lips. I stared out the window. I flashed back to Patrice, in my first grade bathroom. I left my body behind, floating somewhere I couldn't feel. The sky was cloudy, and there were old women wreathed in black making their way into church across the street.

It seemed forever as he did his best to keep me erect, and I willed myself to come, the sloppy inevitable finish, to give him a meal for all the ones he had fed me. When I finally did it was quick and uncomfortable. He collapsed on the floor, wiping my sperm off his chin as he handed me money, muttering, "Cab fare." I grabbed the fifty dollars—much more than a cab would cost—and took the subway home. I felt like a stranger in my parent's hollow hallways, as I stumbled without seeing from my room to the shower, where I scrubbed myself with soap until it stung.

%&$#?@!

Evelyn moved home to Kentucky without bothering to let me know. A week later, I turned nineteen. One day, while going to the bathroom, I saw a small red sore. I started to cry. Evelyn's good-bye gift to me was cash and some horrible STD, maybe even AIDS. It seemed like poetic justice if I ended up with the virus that had killed off most of my father's old clients.

I was scared and trembling when I told my parents I needed to see a doctor.

"Well your annual checkup is in two weeks, so that's perfect," Mom said, checking her date book.

"You don't understand. I need to see one now." I avoided her eyes.

"Do you want to talk about it?" Dad asked.

"Please, just set up an appointment," I said.

"Okay," Dad relented. "We can do patient confidentiality this time."

My pediatrician, Dr. Brancaccio, had died that year of lung cancer. He was a sarcastic, pockmarked, chain-smoking gay man with thinning, bleached-blonde hair. I knew he would have understood. He had made my early doctor visits funny and stress-free. He jokingly snapped at my parents and listened carefully to me.

He had seen me through earaches, hepatitis shots, and the awkward years of puberty. He made sure I was healthy while he smoked away his life between patients. Mom shook her head when she told me about his packed funeral, looking perplexed and horrified.

"He had been through lung cancer once before. It went away, but he just kept smoking." Her voice was laced with bitterness.

"He knew what he was doing," I said.

"But he was happy." She looked at me in disbelief.

Mom had no idea what was going on with me. Did I look happy to her?

A new doctor was in Dr. Brancaccio's office and my appointment was with him. The waiting room was eerie—the same photos of laughing babies lined the walls; the same toys I had played with when I was five years old were messily strewn over the maroon carpet.

"Hi, I'm Dr. Perez. Come on in," a man in a long white lab coat said, opening his door. He looked younger and fresher faced than Dr. Brancaccio. He had a wedding ring. I was terrified he'd think I was a total homo. I wanted to explain I was after fame and I'd gotten horribly sidetracked. Most of all, I didn't want him to see my diseased dick.

I nervously entered the office I had walked into for checkups all eighteen years of my life. The walls were covered with a mural of a rainforest. When I was little I loved to search for animals hidden among the leaves to distract myself from syringes.

"How are you?" Dr. Perez asked, sitting behind Dr. Brancaccio's desk.

"It's weird, being in here," I said, still looking around the room.

"A lot of people say that." He smiled. "I hear he was a really great guy."

"He was," I blurted, suddenly feeling like I was going to cry.

"Was your sexual partner a man or a woman?" Dr. Perez asked calmly.

"A man." I blushed.

"What did you engage in?" came the next carefully impartial question.

"Oral sex." I looked down at the floor, feeling my face glow red.

"Did you use protection?"

"No." I winced.

"Well, let's take a look," Dr. Perez said, rising from his desk and coming around toward me expectantly. I unbuttoned my pants and he knelt down. For a startled second I feared he would go down on me too, and I shriveled in shock. He looked me over and smiled. "Looks like a minor scratch," he said. "You've been going a little rough on yourself, that's all."

"I still want a blood test."

"Full blood test? HIV too?" he asked.

Evelyn's teeth could have scraped me during his sloppy blowjob. I paused, pulling up my pants, happy with Dr. Perez's preemptory diagnosis, but still not completely convinced.

"Yes," I said.

Luckily, I got my negative results a week later. By that time the sore had gone away, but my boozing had escalated to match Evelyn's. I took on his worldly manner, name-dropping, and wasting what little money I had like a millionaire. When I wasn't drunk or pretending to be rich, I spent my time writing feverishly. I was determined to prove Evelyn wrong. I could be a straight, successful writer without selling my body. I sent out short stories to every literary journal I could find online, but all I got back were rejections. Drowning my disappointment in handles of Jim Beam, I spent more and more nights raging at parties on Allen Street, acting as sleazy as Evelyn had made me.

10
All I Want for Hanukah

"I don't know who I am anymore," I sobbed while Mom held my shaking frame.

"Sweetie, what's wrong?" she asked.

"Why doesn't Dad love me?" I hiccupped.

"What's going on in there?" My father knocked on my bedroom door.

"Go away! I hate you!" I shouted.

I had been chugging the Jim Beam stashed behind my pillow and wondering where that bastard Evelyn was. I was angry and upset thinking of the way he'd used me. I blamed Dad's dicks, the giant penis paintings that he had chosen to spend my childhood hours making. I felt further away from my parents than I had all my life and like I had returned home to find a hostile environment where I was no longer welcome. Their intense involvement turned to scary scrutiny. I was trapped in a childhood bedroom that my drinking habit had grown too big for. I was "behind the bar"—in a place my parents could not invade, speaking a language my mom didn't speak, in an underground my dad couldn't crawl into. In a cave I would adorn with my own wild, wasted scrawling.

"Let me in this minute," Dad yelled, banging on the door.

"You don't care about me. I don't need you," I cried.

"Hazak, I can't talk to you when you're like this," Mom said.

"Please, don't leave." I tugged at her sweater.

"We'll discuss this with your father in the morning," she said.

But we didn't. When I woke up sober, I felt too ashamed to approach her. Besides, Mom reported everything back to Dad.

After Evelyn left, I compulsively checked Myspace, hoping he might send me a message apologizing or explaining why he'd gone. I had hours to spend online, clicking at random, diving through strangers' worlds for the soothing escapism. There were already Myspace celebs like stripper Tila Tequila and Cunt the Pink Dream, a trashy trannie from L.A. I started adding friends too, telling myself I could also be a cybercelebrity, but really hoping to connect with anybody. I sent messages to a gorgeous green-eyed girl in Toronto and we talked about Paris Hilton, gold shoelaces, and our shared thirst for fame (she assured me it was much easier to achieve as an American); I connected with the bassist of a West Coast band who wore skinny black ties and took photographs of hot girls kissing. In this new cyberfrontier it seemed everyone was able to project a somewhat famous image of themselves, and it was easy to create a network of strangers who could distract me from loneliness and who sometimes seemed closer than real-life friends.

%&$#?@!

I stumbled across Georgina's Myspace page. She had been friends with Melon from my Clinton school days. Back then, Georgina had dark eyes and a long neck, wore ripped stockings and black Doc Martens, and took photobooth pictures before it was cool. I had always been drawn to her and her gangly awkwardness that promised good things. Now, her photos showed the same depthless eyes, subtle cheekbones, and long honey hair. Her face looked different in each photo. In one, it was round and deliciously bruised, lips forming a peachy pout. In another, she was a pale Geisha in hoop earrings, eyes slanted back with slashes of thick eyeliner, hair straightened, and breasts pushed up by red lace lingerie. I hoped she would be the perfect place to hide from my parents. I started fantasizing about Georgie. I needed a woman's soothing touch to help me forget Evelyn's rough mouth. "Want to have a reunion?" I messaged her.

In just a few, brief messages, Georgie told me her neurotic Catholic mother had moved to Hollywood, where she scored movie soundtracks before having a nervous breakdown. Georgie had inherited the cozy two-bedroom facing Tompkins Square Park, where she had grown up in the constant chaos of her mother's wake. Walking toward her apartment past the park where I had fallen off jungle gyms, I thought my old feelings for her might be the perfect antidote for feeling cheap and dirty, as if Evelyn's comment about me looking like a gigolo would come true.

Georgie opened the door, all blonde curls and brown eyes heavy with black eye shadow and mascara.

"Come on in," she said as we hugged.

"I'm so glad I quit the Toe Zone," she sighed over a joint in her bedroom.

"What's that?" I asked.

"It's a private club for guys with foot fetishes. I wore stilettos, and these old, rich businessmen would do coke off my feet and ask me to kick them in the mouth. I haven't really been in touch with any of my friends. They got really mad at me when I worked there, but it paid for City College," she said, sounding almost sage. "I met this sixty-one-year-old guy named Marvin. He bought me a TV and five pairs of Jimmy Choos. But when he wanted to fly me to Paris ..." She laughed as she finished her sentence by snipping at the air with imaginary scissors and fake vomiting over the side of her bed.

"Wow, that's about the same age as my dad," I said and laughed with her.

"Yeah, it was just getting disgustingly crazy, so I quit. Now I can focus on acting again and I'm working at a health food store. Which smells like horrible little hippies, but isn't full of as many freaks." She shrugged and said, "All beautiful people have scars."

Our knees touched.

"Guess what? I'm dating my first boy in a year." Georgie said. "I was sort of a lesbian for a while. Except for that weird threesome with — well, you know who." And I did. But they will remain anonymous, for legal reasons.

"This rich alcoholic guy sucked my dick for fifty dollars, but I'm straight," I confessed.

"I know you are, silly," she said.

A few weeks later the boyfriend was dumped, and Georgie and I were flirty and inseparable. She was sharp and wicked, giggling with me endlessly as we rolled in the clean sheets of her big Ikea bed, surrounded by dried, pressed flowers and oil paintings by her dead uncle hanging from the ochre walls of her bedroom.

We devoured movies and joints, watching *Natural Born Killers*, *Pink Flamingos*, Andy Warhol's *Heat*. When I was around Georgie—in her vintage coats with flopping sheepskin collars, her oversized sunglasses, and her crooked smile—I felt just like the wonderfully fucked-up characters we saw on screen. She made damaged look good. And she made me feel better.

While it was considered cute for girls like Georgie to casually hook up with girls, it was controversial for straight guys to have a gay blow job in their past. I still felt unclean, as if there was a depraved, perverted part of me that thrived on humiliation and force. It made me feel confidently sexy again to know Georgie still wanted to be with me. Georgie also thrived on fame, and it dominated our conversations, the word lingering on my lips as I listened to Leonard Cohen on the stoned walks home late at night from her house to my parent's place. Every time I slipped my key into their lock, I felt I was closing a door, not opening one.

%&$#?@!

Ricardo, a pale, pockmarked, rail-thin Dominican boy that Evelyn had fucked, was interning at the swank Robert Miller Gallery on 27th Street. I ran into him at an opening with friends. The neighborhood was filled with the rich and famous and now I knew someone on the inside.

"You're such a party boy. No wonder Evelyn liked you," Ricardo said. "We'll make you a star."

"My friend Ricardo is going to introduce me to all these high-art people," I told my father. I wanted to impress Dad, who still made ceramic pots in his studio and sold them at Mom's synagogue—though he still refused to attend any services. The designs were now floral and Grecian, not phallic.

"Why don't you get a job at Duane Reade? They're hiring. You left Bennington because you were depressed just so you could run around till all hours of the night?" he asked.

"It's called networking."

"It's called bullshit," he retorted.

"No wonder art dealers don't care about my dad. He's such a square Jew," I fumed on the phone with Ricardo.

"Don't worry, darling, my connections will love you," he exclaimed.

I worked in SoHo, at a place that only showed artwork of buildings in New York. The Empire State and Chrysler buildings, along with pigeons and bridges hung on the walls. I was getting paid ten dollars a day, and my boss always came in hours late for work, shouting, "We have a new Times Square," sending the small staff into a flurry of pretend activity. I was learning everyone in New York pretended to be busier than they actually were.

I had been looking forward to the Robert Miller Gallery Christmas Party for months. Ricardo insisted it was going to be my introduction into high society. There was no way I was going to light Hanukah candles with my parents and eat Mom's latkes. I planned to hit the gallery bash in style, then cab to Georgie's house for a stoned after-party.

Ricardo came to pick me up, and I made him wait, uncomfortably, in my parent's living room while I put the finishing touches on my costume. I emerged in a black sweater hung with plastic diamonds and a giant white fur coat. I decided it would impress the gallery elite if I came looking like a piece of art myself.

"You look like a homeless schizophrenic," Dad chuckled, as I nervously checked out my getup in the living-room mirror.

"I think that's a woman's sweater," Mom said, lighting Hanukah candles. "Why don't you stay for dinner?"

"I look too good," I glared.

"Everyone will spot you," Ricardo decided.

As our cab crawled by the East River on our way to the Miller Townhouse on Central Park East, Ricardo looked pensive while he hummed "Santa Baby" under his breath. Snow came down thickly and I shivered inside the cab with both cold and excitement.

When Ricardo and I arrived, the door opened and the giant glamorous apartment sprawled before us. I was awed by a drawing room filled with original works by Picasso and Pollock, macho painters that made my father's collection of naives and rescued garbage pieces seem pathetic. A small tuxedoed swing band played Louie Armstrong's "A Kiss to Build a Dream On." In the center of the drawing room, framed by a giant glass window looking onto Central Park, was the bar.

"Ricardo, welcome," crowed a plain-faced woman in black.

"Darling," Ricardo said and hugged her.

"Are you together?" she asked, smiling at me.

"Just for the night," I replied and smiled back, realizing too late this made me sound like the way I felt: a paid escort. The only way to gain entry to the luxurious life I craved appeared to be by flaunting my youth, looks, and body: Six feet, two inches and gaunt; grey eyes, often sad and fugitive; full lips and smooth chin. I was described as beautiful more often than handsome. Accentuated by my feminine clothes, I pushed the boundaries of androgyny—the lure of a pretty boy with shadows in his gaze. When I walked into rooms people noticed me. Both women and men smiled at me in the streets, desire parting their careless lips. I knew my ragged looks gave me power, but I wasn't comfortable with it, didn't know how much I was willing to use it to get what I wanted.

"Oh," the woman's smile slipped and she cleared her throat. "Well, enjoy."

"She's an opera singer," Ricardo said. He was already whispering a diatribe as we made a beeline for the bar. "The mother is the fat lady in pearls. The father is gay and lives with his lover in France."

I quickly sucked up vodka.

"Gin and tonic," Ricardo said to the bartender. Then he whipped around, gushing "Darling!" as he introduced me to a blank, Botox-faced woman in a purple cocktail dress. "This is Stephanie. She used to be friends with Michael 'Party Monster' Alig."

She nodded. "Ricardo, I need a fucking drink. My husband is being so annoying."

"Boring husband. Start hustling," Ricardo said, pushing me toward her.

"Where did you come from?" she sneered as she motioned to the bartender, then gulped a goblet of red wine as soon as it was in her hands.

"The Lower East Side."

"Oh," she scoffed. "When did you move there?"

"I was born there."

"Oh my God." She smiled as much as her face muscles would allow, gesturing animatedly. "I used to go to so many coke bars there in the early '90s. They were all clustered around Tompkins Square Park. My girlfriends and I would get all fancy and snort in sketchy back rooms."

"Sounds like my old hood," I smiled. "I used to wave 'hi' to hookers on my way to kindergarten."

After some cozy schmoozing with Alig girl, I was feeling like a tart in the best way. Some indescribable shine had rubbed off on me, as if just being in the presence of fame and money lifted me up. I soaked it in with the open brain of a newborn, noting styles of speech, ways of dress. As if careful mockery could make me important too. Yet there was also a rebellious, stubborn streak in me that saw the great illusion in all this—that part of my heart that hummed with hunger for any-thing of substance. Ricardo, suddenly at my shoulder, apparently had no such apparatus.

"Dinner is served," he announced dryly. "You should do her," he whispered in my ear as we stood up, staggering to the buffet, where waiters hovered.

After dinner, Ricardo and I weaved our way to the long, low white couch in the living room. The Christmas tree was thirty feet tall, way eclipsing my mother's menorah. A withered, old dandy in an impecca-ble navy blue suit approached us. The gay gleam in his eye reminded me of Evelyn and I choked on my gin and tonic.

"Can I touch your top? I've been eyeing it all night?" he asked me.

"Sure, go ahead." I rolled my eyes. I was hoping to attract a big shot art dealer, not another creepy, old fag. But if everyone else was faking it, so could I. Apparently, the only power in my life came from my penis, and it felt good to be in control of something.

"Marvelous," he croaked as he fondled my sweater. "What do you do?" he asked, grinning and sliding into the place beside me.

"I'm a writer," I said.

"Adorable. How fucking original," exclaimed the dandy. He had stuffing stuck in his teeth.

"He writes tacky poetry," Ricardo interjected. "What do you do?"

"I've seen it all," he said. "I've been head chef for this family for over twenty years. I met everybody. Liza. Everybody. Saw the Factory years, the disco years. Cocaine, champagne, blow jobs."

"I'll be in the smoking room," I said, getting up. A fawning queer cook wasn't going to get me very far.

I grabbed another Bombay and tonic at the bar, then went to the bathroom to roll a joint. When I pushed the door open, the old gay chef was pissing into a gold-plated toilet bowl.

"Sorry," I muttered.

"That's okay," he looked back at me over his shoulder and winked. I slammed the door.

After midnight, the party started thinning.

"We cannot be the last losers here," Ricardo whispered frantically in my ear, grabbing the half-full glass of top-shelf booze out of my greedy grasp and pushing me toward the coat rack.

Later, my body buzzed with energy as we smoked a goodnight joint. I was addicted to the glamour, even though in the back of my head I knew I was a penny picked off the streets, polished and placed in the drawing room. Ricardo was already talking about the upcoming party at SoHo House. Then there was the gala across from Ground Zero for Renee Cox, the black artist who photographed herself naked as Jesus.

"You're coming with me, right?" he asked. "Everyone loved you tonight."

"Yeah, I'll be your official party buddy." I smiled.

"Great." Ricardo shook my hand like we'd just made a business deal.

After Ricardo dropped me off in a cab downtown, I walked in the door at Georgie's party. She was surrounded by people drinking and smoking. Still, her face shone when she saw me. I grinned back, feeling like I oozed sophistication in a way her other admirers didn't.

"I've been waiting for you all night. Come with me," she slurred as she hugged me close, taking my hand. Stoned, drunk, and feeling like fooling around, I followed her eagerly to the bathroom where a model-skinny girl was kneeling on the floor.

"I want you to make out with her," Georgie said, shutting the door. "It will be hot."

The model and I tongued, teeth occasionally bumping, Georgie rubbed the back of my stoned head, and then drew one of my hands toward her crotch. My fingers pushed past her panties. We both gasped as I slid them inside her for the first time. The model gave a bony grin and lay back on the floor, small tits slipping out of her silky top. I ground my erection against her crotch, my fingers still caught in the wet warmth of Georgie. I stopped making out with the model to lick Georgie's mouth, but Georgie jumped in where I had left off. The girls moved away from me and as I stared, jealous and surprised, they lay down on the tiled bathroom floor and started fingering each other. Turned on, I tried to join. Georgie pulled me in, but the model groaned "get rid of him," -without even looking at me.

"Sorry." Georgie pushed me away in the same motion.

"Fuck you!" I got up hard and unsteady and wobbled out, slamming a bathroom door for the second time that evening. I had been a spectator on the sidelines all night, and though I was prepared to grovel at the altar of the rich and powerful, I felt no need to stand by while Georgie had fun without me. I wanted Georgie alone, not with anyone else. I thought Georgie had broken up with her boyfriend for me. I felt strangely old-fashioned, stuck in a world of young, sexed-out creatures where anything went and where flirty Myspace messages masqueraded as real connections. I stormed home through the snow and ice, ignoring traffic signs, slipping by speeding cars and angry shouts.

When I got to my parent's house, I was so drunk my vision came in flashes. I saw all the lights on in their living room. Masks. Hallway. Blood smeared on the floor. I walked right past it. Boozed up, I locked myself in my room and passed out.

%&$#?@!

"Hazak! Wake up, there's been a medical emergency." Dad banged on my door the next morning.

"What happened?" I asked, letting him in.

"Your mother is in St. Vincent's Hospital. She fainted last night in the bathroom."

"Is she okay?"

"She'll be fine. They're pumping her full of fluids intravenously. I told her a million times: 'You're going through a rough menopause, bleeding all over the place. You need to see a doctor.' And the woman doesn't listen. We'll visit her tonight."

But I didn't visit her that night. Instead, I splurged on a $60-gram of cocaine. Having my mom hooked up to an IV made me feel like I needed a steady drip too. I bought a handle of Jim Beam and threaded my way through Alphabet City pedestrian traffic. I passed a homeless man wrapped in tattered oriental rugs, drunk NYU girls in Santa hats and Vincent Gallo. I was desperate to escape inside of Georgie and knew she wouldn't be able to resist the combination of cocaine and whiskey. I lit a Marlboro Red, walking through snow flurries and already seeing Christmas trees, tied up with twine, their branches broken and dirty, waiting on curbs to be picked up and thrown away, digested by the masticating metal of garbage truck hatches.

Georgie opened the door—looking smart and sexy, one eyebrow raised nonchalantly—and draped herself around me as a hello. Pretty soon we were pouring refills, blowing lines, and scribbling girls getting screwed on napkins on her living-room floor.

"You were jealous last night, weren't you?" she asked, rings of white powder around her nostrils.

"I was. You're supposed to be my bitch."

"You sound so sexy when you say that," she purred.

Leaning in, she licked my lips, which were numb from the cocaine. We climbed onto her couch, and she took off her shirt, bare breasts full. We started kissing deep, tongues together, teeth tugging at lips. I pulled off her pants, then mine, wanting to be completely naked with her. Her body warmed me after the cold, the soft hair between her legs rubbing against me like a plea. Her hands expertly tugged me to full stiffness as I sucked and swallowed her nipples again and again.

"Does this feel good?" She grinned into my cheek.

"So good, so good, so good," I said.

"How about this?" She licked down my chest and stomach, taking half my length into her mouth at once.

Through the hazy pleasure I had weird flashbacks to Evelyn. I didn't want another mouth on my cock. When she started licking my ass, I pushed her head away.

"I want to be inside you instead."

"You're so straight," she replied, nibbling my balls. "But I don't have a condom."

"I won't come unless I fuck you," I slurred.

"Just enjoy this," she said and petted my chest.

"I want to fuck." I pulled her up and forced her to kiss me, but as soon as our lips parted, she rolled away, walked into her bedroom, and closed the door. Still, I jerked off on her couch—covered in release and smiling as the sun came up.

%&$#?@!

Georgie tiptoed around me after our hookup, making jokes about what had happened, implying it was a funny drug- and alcohol-fueled mistake. I desperately wanted more of her body. She quickly developed a crush on an older lesbian who'd had a turn as a child actor in an indie film. Georgie contacted her on Friendster, the already sadly deserted social networking site of 2004, and started an Internet flirtation.

"She's an actress like me, she gets it," Georgie gushed to me on the phone as I glumly stared at the walls of my room where I was now trapped, "Aren't you happy? I'm meeting her for coffee."

"Have fun," I replied, hanging up, furious.

Pretty soon Georgie was dating indie girl, claiming they were "in love." I kept hoping this was another phase with Georgie; as an actress she liked to play different roles. Her new girlfriend was in AA and Georgie dramatically quit drinking, smoking, and most surprising of all, puffing the fat joints she used to look forward to after hard days on her feet as a health food cashier. Whenever I called her she seemed distant or wouldn't pick up at all. As soon as I had gotten naked with her she had no need for me anymore. It didn't seem anyone did. Love and sex were things that I decided to hate, projecting a cold, disgusted attitude no one could penetrate. It hid a heart easily breakable and a crushing fear that I was deeply damaged, unlovable.

Georgie and I went from being together all the time, talking long into the night about poetry, acting, and where our lives were headed, to cautious phone calls. My fantasy of having her as a girlfriend was over, and I concentrated all my energy on dancing at luxury hotels and guzzling at open bars with Ricardo. But the more we boozed and schmoozed, the more removed Ricardo got. Though I strove for celebrity, more and more I secretly craved human connection. Ricardo was the other way around. I knew fame, money, status, success were more important to him than the sacrifices real relationships demanded. He would sell me out the second it no longer paid to have my presence around. The people I had been introduced to over and over still called me "Kazaam"—a blatant bastardization of my name they clearly thought clever.

Ricardo was going back to Toronto for the summer. My parental patience clock was ticking. Mom was safely back from her brief hospital stay, but the fact that I had never visited had made even her sweet soul shrivel from me. I hadn't made lasting ties to any of the sweaty hands I shook at the Gansevoort, Matthew Marks, or Marquee. Without Ricardo I was back on the streets, my name not on any guest lists.

11
America's Next Top Idol

"You think your fancy friends care about you? You think they'll help pay your rent?" Dad yelled at me.

"What are you talking about?" I snarled at him.

"I'm sick of the way you're treating this family, gallivanting around with shallow snobs. It's time to buckle down and get a real job. From now on, you're to pay me sixty dollars a week for staying under my roof," my father said.

"How am I supposed to save for the down payment on my own apartment if you're taking all my money? Don't you want me to move out? Can't I just cook you guys dinner once a week?" I tried to negotiate.

"No, I want cash." He folded his arms.

"Don't you get enough money from Mom? I'm not paying for your fucking paintbrushes," I told him.

"This is a final decision," he intoned.

My father was right. Chic party hopping wasn't very lucrative. I ended up spending most of my money on cabs and Marlboro Reds. If Georgie had cared enough, I would have left my parents' house and stayed with her. In my wild, abandoned fantasies, in skintight pants and leather boots, I was too pompous to get a basic job, believing I was above it. My fashionable self-hatred turned outward on the world.

I told my parents I would go hand out resumes, but all my accomplishments were too raunchy to put down on paper, and being famous wasn't exactly a job you could apply for in Human Resources. I sat in Roosevelt Park, reading day after day, hoping I would get discovered and knowing how unrealistic and absurd this expectation was. The park had long been free of the syringes I used to collect with my father. I remembered the days when he and I would set off into the bare branches together, making a game out of who could collect the most needles in padded gloves. Or was it one of our earliest competitions? Either way, with the help of other community organizers, my father and I had made this soil fertile, spread the first seeds for the park's flowers, which now grew lush and lovely when it was Spring. I watched wealthy white kids my age walk through the now clean paths. My neighborhood was up and coming. What about me? Didn't I, a veteran of these blocks, deserve attention too?

"Have you ever modeled?" A female voice made me look up from *The Philosophy of Andy Warhol (From A to B and Back Again)*. A pretty black woman stood before me, withered leaves piled around her tan leather knee-high boots.

"You have that look," she continued, handing me a card. "Come into my agency and mention me. I think they'd be very interested in meeting you."

"Thanks," I nodded, trying to play it cool, but secretly thrilled. A few shady modeling scouts had stopped me before; I never took them seriously. But this woman was sexy and looked legit. Though I didn't recognize her agency name, the address was a high-rent one on Broadway, a few blocks above Canal Street. It seemed whenever I had given up on fame, my city sent me a sign. There was no such thing as coincidence in the world of celebrity.

When I went in for an appointment I entered a huge loft space with wood floors, busy employees, and a giant conference room where fifty other hopefuls were gathered, watching a glorified documentary about the world of high fashion.

"Hazak Brozgold would look fabulously exotic in print," gushed my interviewer, an anorexic-looking Asian woman with bangs. "On a scale of one to ten, how dedicated are you to being a model?" she asked.

"Eleven," I answered quickly.

"I love that answer! You have too much potential. Let me call my boss and you can chat."

She left the room and a built man in a tweed blazer stomped in.

"We'd like to offer you a contract, but we ask five hundred dollars up front for portfolio fees," he said as we shook hands.

"I don't have any money," I told him.

"Credit card number?" He looked annoyed.

"I don't have a credit card."

"What if I wanted to send you on a shoot right this minute to Rio de Janeiro in Brazil?" he asked angrily. "You need to have your credit card information on you if you want to succeed."

"I haven't even signed anything," I pointed out.

"You won't." He marched out of the room.

What a scam. Still, I left the agency excited. If a bunch of fakes wanted me, I could con someone legit into wanting me too. I decided to pursue a career as a male model. It was a step up from hustler. It wasn't what I really wanted, but the flashiness and flashbulbs appealed to me.

"I'm going to be a model," I told my parents later that day.

"For who? Kmart?" Dad smirked.

Yuvi volunteered to take Polaroids of me. He was still obsessed with being a film director and was happy to have a subject to boss around. In preparation, I got drunk off the Jim Beam still stashed behind my pillows.

"Look angry," Yuvi directed. "Okay, chin up—look toward the light," he said, snapping away and repositioning my wasted limbs.

At six feet, two inches, and 160 pounds, I was all angles. Dressed in vintage designer clothes, I imagined I was bringing a fresh, new style to the fashion game. I looked scruffy and desperate in the pictures, and they stuck out. I started at the top, Googling all the famous agencies in New York and writing down the times for their open calls. Everyone was scouring the masses for the next Tyson Beckford or Kate Moss.

But I always got the same, cold "you're just not right for us at the moment," from polished secretaries two inches too short to stomp down runways. I never saw them take anyone. All the male and female hopefuls left dejected together. I looked down at the ground and hurried away from the pack, humiliated, but trying to look like I was rushing to another gig.

At Next Models, a beefy aspiring male model brought his screaming baby with him. Everyone glared in his direction, and I could tell I wasn't the only one angrily thinking: *Pimp the kid for a contract. Why didn't I do that?* It was always the same shitty experience waiting in pristine and impersonal offices that smelled like Chanel perfume and desperate sweat.

I knew a Polish coke dealer who modeled, found out his agency's address on Broadway and 24th Street, and went up there.

"Excuse me, can I drop off my photos with you?" I went up to the secretary, a squat, angry-looking woman with glasses and disheveled grey hair. She took one look at me from behind her desk and then a purple web of veins rose in her round cheeks, her small lips twisted together, and saliva spewed in a wet arc around me as her whole being contorted in disgust.

"Get out of here!" she screamed, as if I was too hideous to stay another second.

The last-resort agency on my list after weeks of "no thank-you's" was shabbier than the others, and the secretary seemed confused when I walked in and announced I had an appointment with B.J.. She spent a few minutes on the phone, while I waited in an uncomfortable chair, taking in the ratty carpeting, the walls cracked with water stains. Perhaps dilapidation was now *de rigueur*?

As I sat there, a tall, willowy boy came in; he had thin blond hair cut asymmetrically over one eye.

"I did Ecstasy with Sean Lennon last night," he announced to the secretary, kicking one leg back at the knee and flexing the toe of his pointy Capezio.

"Oh, Cookie," she exclaimed. "You're so bad."

They proceeded to have a hushed dialogue punctuated by squeals. Had I wandered into a recruiting agency for prostitutes? I restudied the too-glossy photos of half-naked male and female "models."

The secretary's phone lit up and she eyed me warily as she listened to the voice on the other end.

"Looks fresh enough," she reported, then turned to me. "B.J. will see you now."

B.J. was a middle-aged black man with sunken cheeks. He reclined in his tiny, cluttered office. His eyes were rolled back in his head so I could only see the whites, and I thought he looked like he was smashed on heroin. Growing up surrounded by junkies, I had learned to tell what drugs people were on. B.J.'s outfit consisted of one long, grey sweat suit, and he wore a pink bandana over his head like a fashion-of-fending gang member.

"Did you bring pictures?" He drew out every syllable, trying to get his tongue around them. I smiled and handed him my Polaroids.

"You can sit on the couch," he gestured.

"Oh, thanks." I said, grinning and letting the nervousness show in my face. I already knew this was a shady deal, but I didn't want to let on. Evelyn had taught me that pervs like this sensed fear. I had to lull B.J. into a false sense of security so I could use him, then lose him. At nineteen, I thought that was how the world worked.

"Take off your shirt," B.J. drawled.

I stood up awkwardly, purposefully letting my hands shake a little as I undid the buttons of my long-sleeved flannel. B.J. glanced up and down like an appraiser, from my collarbone to the abs I had been trying to cultivate.

"You're a little avant-garde. You need to work out more. You can put your shirt on again," came the verdict.

I sat back down on his couch, smiling in a way I hoped made me look like an innocent farm boy from Nebraska instead of the formerly dangerous Lower East Side.

"I like you," he said, as if this were a generous admission. "Which is why I'm telling you, you have no future in couture. We're having a showcase for one of our bands later—we have a hand in every honey pot here—I can introduce you to the people in the TV and commercial department. At five."

I grinned as I walked out of our appointment. Even if I'd slept my way to the bottom, at least I was going somewhere. I thought if I just flirted with B.J., I could string him along and get at least a few photo shoots and quick cash out of it. I rushed home to tell my parents the spectacular news. Landlord Dad would be appeased.

"I met this guy who thinks I'd be a great commercial model," I announced to Mom, who was home from the hospital and flattening ripe bananas for a Dominican-style pastelone filled with ground turkey, since Dad didn't eat beef. She liked practicing Spanish at the Essex Street Market and dancing to world music while she prepared family dinners.

"Is he legitimate?" she asked, not looking up from her cooking.

"Of course," I said, annoyed she'd pinpointed the problem with B.J. right away.

"Did you make sure?" she asked.

"Do you think a fraud is the only agent that would want me?"

"I just think you should make sure," she said, stirring the filling.

"I have an appointment at five. I'm leaving," I announced.

"But I made dinner," Mom said, as I rushed out the door.

I found B.J. in his office surrounded by a group of surly underage male models, glowering at each other and vying for a space nearest him.

He was sipping vodka with Tropical Snapple from a tall shot glass, and he grinned when I entered. It was becoming clearer that these lanky boys were his sex toys, and he pimped them out to cheap photographers pushing false fame.

I felt sad for them while they scowled at me, hating me, thinking I would take their stall in this stable. I wondered if B.J. was just perpetuating a perverse cycle—if he had once been like these young boys, gathered around a lonely con man hungry for sex.

Later, in a cab with two typical industry frauds from B.J.'s agency, we whizzed over to a sound studio in the Meatpacking District. The woman had pulled back hair, a Prada bag, and chain-smoked Parliament Lights. The man was quiet and reassuring, with a friendly, fleshy face. They were a good cop, bad cop duo to lure potential human meal tickets.

"You can't just tag along all night," the woman spat at me. "We're here to work you know."

"Don't worry. I'm strictly with B.J.," I smiled.

She winced and turned away. I was going behind the scenes of a large-scale scam.

The soundstage for the performance was all black, the first three rows packed with a gaggle of prepubescent girls taking photos with digital cameras and cell phones. I sat on the floor in front of B.J.'s chair. He put his hands on my shoulders.

The lights went down and girls started screaming. Two short, cheaply dressed preteens marched on stage in a spotlight followed by chubby backup dancers. I was strangely impressed with the lengths that had been taken to feed this dark flipside to being famous. In the "real" world, thousands of people lived and breathed this, performed on these stages with phony backup dancers and sham fans. I could easily fuck my way to fake fame, and my morbid curiosity made me want to see it, front row, in every gritty detail.

I sat through the bad tween pop ballads as B.J. massaged my shoulders in the dark. Finally, the lights came up, the crowd filed out, and I found myself alone on an empty Meatpacking District street with B.J. and a baby-faced boy model who was glancing nervously down at his ringing cell phone. He looked even younger than Yuvi—fifteen years old at most.

"It's my mom," he said. "She gets worried when I'm out this late." He glanced at B.J..

"Oh please," B.J. huffed, rolling his eyes. The vodka on his breath came clear across the chilly night air. He turned to me.

"His mommy is so overprotective. Always blowing up the cellie, not letting him go to castings, keeping his career in check. Ridiculous. Let's go back to the agency. There's a VH1 party at Stereo you're coming to with me."

"I should get home. My mom will be really mad." The boy blushed.

"Well, don't forget you have a shoot bright and early," B.J. sighed. "I have a photographer who thinks you're crazy sexy."

"How old is he?" I asked as the boy ran off into the night.

"Fourteen. He has a lot of potential," B.J. snarled, walking quickly ahead. I hated his back.

When we got to the office, it was deserted. B.J. flipped the TV to *American Idol*. I watched too. Success was an American pastime. Everyone wanted to be a star, a somebody. Reality television dominated every airwave. YouTube sensations crawled their way out of the muck into the news and then on to hosting gigs at state college parties the nation over, to mall openings, to reality shows about former reality stars. There was a galaxy of desperation all over America, a sea of people who thought they should be famous just for being themselves. I was drowning in the roar.

"I just love this show," B.J. drawled, then went to his office.

When he sashayed out ten minutes later to bade me enter, I could tell he'd just shot up. His drooping eyes were almost closed, legs slow and unsteady, hands floppy and gesturing through the air around him like a drowning swimmer. He fell into his chair and carefully removed a big bottle of Smirnoff, a fresh Tropical Snapple, and two glasses from his desk drawer.

As the clock struck midnight, B.J. began making calls on loudspeaker, talking exaggeratedly to bodiless voices.

"Don't wear youa fuckin' sweata suit," an Italian-accented man blared into the room. My cell went off—Georgie on the caller ID. I wanted to tell her I missed her, that I was stuck in a seedy underworld and not sure what I was doing there. I knew she would instantly understand and know how to puncture this parody with one word, to show me in a second that I was too smart to be where I was.

"Hey, I'm on my way to a private VH1 party at Stereo, can I call you later?" I said when I picked up. That would show her for ditching me for indie girl.

B.J. held up a black thong and a pair of prefaded jeans. "I need to change. Do you mind?"

I shook my head no. B.J. stripped while I averted my eyes.

"Really? Call me back, OK? I miss you." Georgie, still on the line, sounded startled and hurt in my ear.

"Sure," I said, clicking my phone shut.

After I hung up B.J. quickly ushered me out of the office, but not before I had filled an empty Snapple bottle entirely with vodka. If he thought getting me inebriated was going to make me easier to manipulate, he had picked the wrong drunkard to fuck with.

"Who was that on the phone?" he asked suspiciously.

"A girl," I sullenly replied.

"So what are you into?" he asked, a knowing smile across his face.

"What do you mean?"

"Boys or girls?"

"I'm into money," I said coldly.

After seeing the way he acted with that fourteen-year-old boy, B.J. deserved to be played. I wasn't going to be coy and stupid anymore, I was going to be mean.

"I have money," he grinned, as he swiped me into the subway with his Metrocard.

When we emerged soon after, the wind was bitter, cutting up off a dark strip of the Hudson River and forcing its way into my jacket. I kept taking swigs from my vodka-filled Snapple bottle. B.J. wanted me to sign a contract the next day, which basically meant he wanted to have sex. In exchange I could be ushered from disgusting photographer to disgusting photographer, all of them knowing I was a kept man. B.J. turned to me,

"I forgot to warn you," he said. "There's this frat boy I've been plugging, but his girlfriend doesn't know. He gets jealous of a pretty, new face—he beat up another boy last week."

"He can go fuck himself," I said and shrugged.

I wanted easy money, but I'd already passed my limit with Evelyn. Even with women, anal sex completely turned me off. I was not letting anybody touch my ass or sell my body in a harem of hustlers, which included kids younger than my little brother.

When we got to Stereo, the club was packed. B.J. nodded at the big bouncers in dark sunglasses and we were whisked past velvet ropes. I doubted this was a VH1 party—there were no cameras, no celebrities; it was a third-rate night for aspiring stars.

I saw a girl I recognized from my "Fame" high school on the lap of a dreadlocked man. She was wasted, half falling on the floor while he groped her tits. The frat boy was sulking in a corner. He looked at me like he was about to start something when B.J. introduced us, but I just smiled and started dancing. I could see pity and disgust in the eyes of the bartenders as I redeemed free drinks from the tickets B.J. handed me, but I was having fun playing the part. At least I had found a way into Stereo, one of the hottest clubs in the Meatpacking District.

Tables were littered with liquor bottles, and there was an orgiastic gluttony in the air. I puffed Marlboro Reds, blowing the smoke in B.J.'s face, while I laughed at the glowering frat boy.

"Give me another drink ticket, asshole," I whispered in B.J.'s ear.

"What's wrong with you?" B.J. was starting to look annoyed.

I hated him. His predatory instincts reminded me of Evelyn, and I was tired of feeling like an object. At least Evelyn was a great writer. He had been lonely and admitted it. I got a whiskey at the bar.

"What's that?" B.J. asked.

"Smell it, bitch," I said, pushing it under his nose.

He did, recoiling, his face contorting in disgust.

"It stinks," he said.

"Yeah, just like you," I hiccupped.

I was beginning to black out, the strobe lights making me dizzy. The music sounded far away. Afraid B.J. would slip me a roofie and rape me; I disappeared in the crowd, shoving my way toward the door. Outside in the cold night air, I laughed as I stumbled home.

When I signed onto Myspace the next day, hungover, I had a message from B.J.: "CALL ME 2 SET UP UR TEST SHOOT." I deleted it and eagerly clicked on the next item in my inbox from Greg, a men's handler at Wilhelmina, a high-powered agency. I had e-mailed him my photos months ago with some of my short stories, because I thought they might make me stand out. Shocked, I read that Greg liked my potential fiction and wanted to have drinks. I was suspicious he might be another shady sugar daddy who wanted to use me, but his agency's status intrigued me.

"Why do you want to waste your time modeling dude?" Greg asked, a few days later, as we sat in a dingy bar off Union Square. Greg was tan and toned in designer clothes and had a true southern California surfer drawl underneath his poised business persona. He was obviously straight and instantly made me feel comfortable; I knew he was there because he was interested in my writing, not sucking my dick. In my duffel bag I had brought printed pages of a short story I had started about a ménage a trois turned homicide on a luxury cruise.

"I thought modeling would be easy money." I shrugged.

"Look where it got you. B.J. is an industry joke, a real fucking creep, man. Your short story wasn't bad. You could either run around New York being just another crazy cute city kid or you could sit down and write a fucking novel," Greg advised, reading through my work.

I was stunned and elated. After all the rejections and whoring myself out for fame, a handler at one of the top modeling agencies in New York was telling me I was worth something. All my wishing paid off for this moment. Taxi cabs whirred by me when I left him, horns lifting into hymns. Clouds moved from fast to blurring above the lights of high buildings. Walking home down Broadway I moved with untamed energy, ducking around pedestrians, my whole body thrown into a slick, strutting stride. The cement sidewalks became wide and solid, and commanded a grandeur that made me smile.

When I got back home I was so excited I started blabbing to Mom as soon as I walked in the door all about Greg from Wilhelmina and what he'd told me about my wonderful words. I volunteered to take a walk with her to fulfill her iced coffee craving.

"It's like someone is finally giving me direction," I gushed.

"I'd be careful if I were you," Mom said softly.

"What do you mean?"

"Well, some of these modeling people might have other motives. Are you sure he doesn't want sex?" she asked.

"He's not gay. I'm not gay. Don't you think I can tell the difference?" I was shocked. "I've met enough assholes who want to use me by now. Who only care about my body, who want to fuck me. It makes me sick."

I couldn't believe my mother was trying to protect me—too late—from the one person who hadn't wanted to screw me. Then I realized I had felt this way about her for a long time. For almost my whole life, a part of me had hated her for solving all her client's problems in her orange office filled with plants, but unable to fix me. I also desperately wanted to sit on her comfortable couch and tell her everything. Except now we were paused in front of a bashful barista, Mom staring at me, her hazel eyes full of worry. As she opened her mouth to speak, I thought finally that she would offer her expert advice and help me. She had heard my honest outburst, the pleading rise at the end of my sentences that screamed: Save me!

"I'll buy you an iced coffee with lots of milk and sugar," she offered.

12
Royal Affair

"Hazak, I have left New York for good. Through all of the highways, the byways I've traveled, through all of the side streets and alleys of sin, through all that's been heard, nothing sinks quite as low as the prominent statements of prominent men." Winky sent me a mixed-up poetic Myspace message. Wondering how she had found me, I clicked on her profile. It revealed a raven-haired fourteen-year-old girl who had photos of herself, pouting, in low-cut designer dresses. She had her location listed as London, New York, Los Angeles.

"I suppose I'm a wine-swilling ghost then," I typed back.

"She always said she likes it slow. But he didn't like to stand still," came her response.

How did she know me? She was friends of friends of friends. After days of debating whether or not to continue what seemed like another pathetic Internet encounter, Winky started leaking into my sleep. I wrote to her again.

"Hey Baby, last night I had a strange dream that you and I were looking at a giant book, which was a collection of portraits of people who had started on Myspace and then become world-renowned. We were looking through it, laughing, in an airy mansion in the Caribbean with all white walls."

Winky quoted The Smiths in her messages: "You can pin and mount me like a butterfly." When I told her I was a Smiths fan, she wrote that front man Morrissey was her "best friend." I imagined Winky and me having an illegal affair while partying with Moz. Her blend of bravado and vulnerability turned me on. I tried to convince myself that age didn't matter. Dad was fifteen years older than Mom. But the truth was I was a depressed, twenty-year-old alcoholic flirting with immature, manipulative jailbait online. She was going to start ninth grade at the elite Professional Children's School on the Upper West Side and we exchanged phone numbers.

Winky called me from L.A , where her sixteen-year-old big sister had just gotten out of a luxe rehab center for cocaine.

"I flew out to be with her, but she's been shopping with Mary Kate all the time. It's lonely in Cali," she breathed over the phone.

"It's lonely in New York, too," I said.

Yuvi, sixteen, was making short films. We bonded over similar artistic passions. He was becoming my famed partner-in-crime.

"You're going to be somebody," he reassured me when Dad told me, "You're a waste of everyone's time. You have grandiose, unrealistic goals that you'll never reach. You're entitled, lazy, and I'm sick of seeing you laying around my house."

It enraged Dad that instead of paying him $60 a week in rent money, I ignored him, coming home late after he had gone to bed and sleeping all day with my door locked. When he cornered me, I would throw him a twenty-dollar bill or a few crumpled singles, staring him in the eyes and imagining his slow death, a superior smirk on my face.

Being immature and close to our respective siblings helped bridge the age gap between Winky and me. My hunger for her worldly boasts blinded me to the rest. After being a lure for creepy men, and now lesbian Georgie, Winky made me feel confident and strangely safe. There was no way a little girl could use me for sex or leak into my heart and then crush it.

After a month of corresponding, she flew to New York. We decided I would meet her by the Virgin megastore in Union Square and we'd go get drunk in Central Park. I was tense about our big date, worried I wouldn't be able to win her over without money. I was petrified that there was a part of me that was too pathetically soft-spoken and shy, an overgrown boy who was gentle by nature. I had tried my best to barricade that part of me off, to bury him. He was weak. When I glimpsed

Winky through the crowds she looked even younger than I expected, with baby chub and underdeveloped breasts, but beautiful, long black hair.

As I headed for the subway she giggled. "We're taking a cab."

"I don't have any money," I admitted.

"I do." she raised her hand to hail a taxi.

On the ride up she talked nonstop in a feigned British drawl, like Madonna's.

"My older sister and I ran away from home before she went to rehab. We threw all our Marc Jacobs in Louis Vuitton bags. Took Daddy's credit card and stayed at the YWCA, doing coke and drinking red wine, dancing all night. Daddy called and told us if we came home right away, he wouldn't tell Mum."

"That's like The Smiths lyric, 'booked myself in at the YWCA,'" I pointed out skeptically.

"Well, that's why we did it." Winky pouted.

As she talked, she compulsively applied lip gloss, pursing her lips and making her eyes bigger when she looked at me. I smiled and nodded, wanting to run my fingers over the curves of her cheek, not caring how much of her jaded words were scripted or real.

I had a bottle of cheap red wine with me that I had poured into a Mott's Apple Juice container for camouflage. We drank it in Central Park on the Great Lawn. She did gymnastics, with her skirt hiked up to reveal lacy black panties, then collapsed on the grass, smoking Parliament 100s.

"You know, when I was five, Lou Reed sang 'Perfect Day' to me to help me go to sleep," she said.

"How do you know him?" I asked.

"He's signed to Daddy's record company, they're old friends."

"I love Andy Warhol. He made the Velvet Underground what they were," I said, hinting and hoping that if her boast about Lou was true, I might be able to wrangle a meeting with the musical genius.

"He would have made you famous, love, but you need a new name," she replied, poking my nose with a pudgy finger.

"What's wrong with Hazak?" I asked.

"It's silly." She wrinkled her nose. "I'm going to call you Royal."

"And that's not silly?" I laughed.

"No, it's lonely."

Wine flowing through me, Winky staring into me, I thought about it. My name had always branded me as an outsider. I had never owned it, never been able to live up to its ancient meaning of strength. I had decided "strong" had many meanings, and equated it to risky, promiscuous, famous. The truth was, I was terrified and felt weak, alone. After burning through high-end gallery parties, sleazy modeling agencies, and extra roles in gay Indie films where no one could remember my heavy Hebrew name, Winky had given me an unforgettable one.

But "Royal Brozgold" rang out as "identity crisis" even louder. I toyed with Royal Bronze Gold, Royal Blue—which Yuvi said sounded like "a retarded porn star." Then one day, after a particularly boring high-school history class, my brother decided to call himself Fury Young. The clear, bland American sound of "Young" balanced the bold, strange first name. I loved it. Fury seemed to suit his somber stare, his peculiar passion for life. I became Royal Young.

"You're not allowed to do that, Yuvi," Winky said, crossing her arms over her chest when I introduced him as Fury. "I gave Royal his new name. You have to earn it."

"Who the fuck says?" Fury challenged her.

"Me. I'm Queen of Sheba," Winky announced.

"More like a spoiled brat," he laughed.

"Your brother is a bore." Winky threw herself around me.

"No, he's not. And if you want to hang out with me, you better get used to him," I said.

"Fine. But now I need Godiva chocolate-covered strawberries," she acquiesced.

Winky paid for strings of cab rides and bottles of wine, supplying me with cigarettes and introducing Royal and Fury to all her rich-kid friends closer to my age. Feeling carefree and monied by proxy beat living with parents who pressured me for rent money—knowing nothing about my new identity that was so far removed from them.

In September, Winky started ninth grade, and my parents found me a part-time job working for a publisher who printed coffee-table books. My boss was an old babysitter of mine. I couldn't wait to be around wordsmiths all day, but when I got there I realized we only published crappy titles that they pushed at drugstore checkout counters—like *Fiesta of Happiness: Be True to Yourself.*

I wasn't surprised when Fury and Winky picked me up one day after work, drunk on whiskey. Her eyes shone with lust as she hugged me.

"I missed you," she whispered, pulling my face down into her long black hair.

"We got trashed at Dorian's penthouse," Fury said, as he walked ahead of us.

I guided Winky down the street while she stumbled into me.

"Let's sit," she said and fell onto a stoop. I sat down next to her, putting an arm over her shoulders.

"I should go home," she whispered and licked my lips. I pulled her closer. The liquor on her breath made my tongue tingle as I tried to keep my hard-on down. I broke away from her, and she wiped smeared pink lipstick from her chin.

"I need to get a cab," she smiled, raising an arm to hail one down at the curb.

I watched, dazed, as she sped away, worried at how turned on I was by this underage pathological liar.

"Did you and Winky just make out?" Fury asked, coming back up to me.

"Yeah," I grinned.

"Weird." He made a gagging face.

"Sexy," I corrected.

"Just be careful. Girls at that age are crazy," he advised.

"I'm coming to get you," Winky laughed into the phone the next day, as I looked out the window at pouring rain.

"Where are you?" I asked nervously.

"First Avenue and Houston Street," she said. "I'm lost—help!"

Even though my parents' apartment sprawled across the entire second floor of our tenement, I was afraid it would look shabby in Winky's eyes. I hoped the fact that it was covered with papier-mâché masks and bright naïve paintings, and had a bathroom papered entirely with silver gum wrappers would seem exotic and appealing to her.

"I'll be right there," I said, hanging up.

I wanted to get her back to my bedroom without my parents seeing. But Mom was monopolizing the kitchen, cooking turkey meatloaf, and spotted us as soon as we came in. I looked at Winky, wondering what Mom would think of her baize Burberry trench covering a miniskirt like a flasher, wet hair matted to her red lips.

"Are you Yuvi's friend?" She smiled at Winky.

"Um," I paused.

"Hi. Royal picked me up in the rain and we're both simply drenched," Winky announced in her British brogue.

"Who's Royal?" Mom looked at me.

"Your son," Winky giggled.

"Which one?" Mom looked confused.

"This charming man," Winky said and slid her arm around my waist.

"Hazak, will your friend be joining us for dinner?"

"I'm not hungry, thank you. I'm an actress," Winky explained.

"We'll be in my room," I said, pushing Winky away down the hall.

"I'm sleepy," she announced, tossing her Burberry raincoat on my floor and curling up on my hastily made bed.

"Don't fall asleep." I lay down next to her.

"Keep me up, then." She moaned as I ran my hands over her breasts. Our lips met and now she tasted like bubblegum. She got on top of me, pinning me down.

"We should stop," I said.

"Hmmm," she breathed, kissing me all over my neck.

"No." I pushed her off me. "My mom is in the next room and you're too young."

"You're too old." She glared at me, rolling off my bed and pulling a Parliament 100 from her Dior handbag.

"You can't smoke in here," I warned, knowing my parents hated the tobacco smell.

"You're so mean," she answered, the cigarette trembling in her lips.

"You can't smoke in my parent's house," I said more gently, trying to wipe away her wet mascara.

"Then I'm leaving." She pulled away.

Even though Winky claimed to have slept with all her male friends, plus Pete Doherty, I didn't think she really knew what she was doing. I had already learned the hard way how much sex could hurt. And already it seemed we needed each other too much.

I met her in Union Square the next day, then we walked to a church near Gramercy Park and sat on the steps smoking Marlboro Reds. I couldn't stop myself from leaning in to smell her hair, wrapping my arms around her and licking her lips between drags of our cigarettes. She told stories of celebrities she met because they were "Daddy's friend." I checked her when her celebrity stories veered toward exaggeration—like when she insisted she was a reincarnation of Edie Sedgwick. Though they did share the same bright burning eyes, wasted wealth, and sadness shellacked with makeup.

I enjoyed showing Winky around the ramshackle Lower East Side, a downtown she had only dreamt of in "never know what you're gonna find there" Velvet Underground lyrics. The neighborhood was in a strange transition, at war with itself. Far from the bedraggled Bowery Lou Reed had written about, seedy landmarks were quickly being replaced by condos. The edge of danger that had originally drawn people to my neighborhood was being whittled away by gentrification. And certainly, stabbings in phone booths and drug overdoses were nothing to miss. Still, I couldn't help but be nostalgic for a time when my corner of Manhattan's meanness kept out the masses and hid a derelict beauty.

I eventually met Winky's older sister in Lizzie Grubman's PR offices on Lafayette Street. Sis was a fast-talking, chain-smoking, coffee-drinking mess. We were all there helping to plan Winky's Warhol-themed debutante debut at the Altman Building. Everyone was frantically stuffing gift bags. Sis stole ten limited edition Paul Frank T-shirts and some energy vitamins, then dragged me out of the building with her to make a getaway. Safely on the street, Sis blithely asked me what my drug of choice was. I knew Winky idolized her, and I answered honestly, "I'm a drinker at heart."

I started feeling protective of Winky. Judging from all the "ur hot" comments she got from random guys on Myspace, I wasn't the only ruthless young man out there who would do anything to get a piece of the fame she advertised. I went from vaguely illegal boyfriend to vaguely illegal bodyguard, exchanging one mismatched role for another.

I met Winky in the Central Park Zoo, when she wanted to go shopping for a gown to wear at Elton John's wedding. I was dragged through Bergdorf's while she tried on outfits whose cost would have helped me pay off my parents for life or feed a hungry village in Sudan for five years.

"I need a simply ravishing dress for Elton's wedding," she announced, descending on the woman selling Yves Saint Laurent.

"I have the perfect thing for you," the salesgirl gushed.

Winky modeled a low-cut purple frock that made her look taller, older, richer.

"Do I look pretty, love?" she asked.

"Very," I said, suppressing the urge to push her onto the dressing room floor, pin her arms down, and slowly strip off her stitches. The salesgirl eyed me suspiciously.

"I love it," Winky spun in front of the mirrors laughing.

"Should I wrap it for you?" The salesgirl asked.

"I'll have to make a date with Daddy to come back," Winky said as her face fell. "Can I put it on hold?"

Winky got into the habit of telling me, "My goal is to ignite you and move on." I laughed this off. It foreshadowed my role as downtrodden artist companion who had only a few minutes' screen time in the reality TV show of her life. Besides, mostly she said it spitefully when I kissed her but wouldn't go further. Then she flew off to Elton's wedding without saying good-bye. I spent my workdays checking her Myspace wall instead of doing spreadsheets, leaving desperate "I miss you" comments until she got back.

"It was fabulous," she drawled, when she finally called me again

"Isn't your father in London? Did he meet you there?" I asked.

"Daddy had a very important meeting in L.A. with Bono. He let me have his credit card to buy my perfect dress. I took a picture and e-mailed it to him. U2 loved it."

I was beginning to realize Winky's extravagant lies escalated whenever she felt deeply wounded by a family constantly too busy for her.

"It was more fun without him anyway. I hung out with Kelly, outside, under all these big tents. Are you coming to my party?"

"Yeah, who's Kelly?" I asked, hurt she hadn't once asked what I had been doing (drinking and looking at her Myspace wall) or said she had missed me.

"Osborne," she replied, hanging up.

I got to Winky's Andy Warhol party early to display my old high-school artwork from LaGuardia on the wall by the Altman bathrooms. She had okayed this display, perhaps wishing for more legitimate downtown grunginess at her fete.

I was shocked to find Winky with another man. I was even more surprised by how much it injured me. I recognized him as a former student from my LaGuardia days where he had been two years behind me. My friends and I used to call him Harry Potter Boy because of his unruly dark hair and round spectacles.

I had convinced Winky to let my brother screen one of his movies starring me on the walls of the ballroom and I rushed over to Fury where he was talking with the sound guy.

"Why the fuck is she with that asshole?" I asked. I still couldn't believe how much seeing her with him cut me.

"She's in high school. Let it go. Your face is going to be projected all over the walls in five minutes," Fury advised.

The film began to roll: a series of campy seductive shots of me in a white wig eating a banana—our Velvet Underground homage—tanning on a roof, a mosquito sucking my blood, the entire film changing color constantly with the "hue" effect on Windows Movie Maker.

Winky pinched Harry Potter Boy and pointed at the screen. They both laughed. She turned and caught me in the crowd staring at her.

"Could you run and get the bartenders some coffee, love?" Winky asked as she sidled up to me for the first time all evening. "They're getting tired setting up."

"What a bitch," I cursed, as I waited in a local deli for five lattes. By the time the party was in full swing I felt like "the help." I feared Winky had been using me all along. I sat in a corner with my brother, glaring at all the wealthy preteens around us. Finally, a downtown party promoter friend showed up and we snuck downstairs to the VIP room to smoke a joint. Halfway through toking, management broke down the door screaming, "Give up the drugs. There are cops outside. Get out!"

My knees buckled as they marched us up the stairs and out of the party in front of all the guests. I averted my eyes as we passed Winky and Harry Potter Boy. Getting a ticket for being drunk in Vermont was one thing. If my parents found out I had been arrested for getting my little brother high, they'd disown me and sit shiva.

"Don't come back," the manager shouted, as we were shoved out a side door onto the barren city street. The police had been only a threat, but there were more angry screams from the manager behind us as we ran, the gold chains around my neck jangling.

Back home, I slipped my key in the back door quietly, but it only opened an inch before the chain lock stopped it. It was 3 a.m. and I was drunkenly swaying and confused.

"Mom and Dad wouldn't lock us out, would they?" I asked Fury.

"I think those assholes just did," he said.

I knew things had gotten bad between us, but this had to be a mistake. We couldn't wake them up stinking of liquor. And where would I take my brother? He looked tired and upset. I couldn't let him sleep on the street. I shoved hard against the door shoulder first, popping the old, rusty chain lock. We slipped inside, I said goodnight to Fury, and staggered to my room, where I fell face down in my bed and passed out.

"You bastard, you broke my fucking door!" Dad screamed at me when I came out of my room the next afternoon, eyes still blurry from sleep.

"You wanted your sons to sleep on the street? We had nowhere to go," I yelled.

"I don't give a shit where you sleep. Your curfew is midnight," Dad shot back. "You're not in bed by midnight, that door is locked, and don't you ever break in again."

I instantly went to check Winky's Myspace. Harry Potter Boy had started leaving sexy comments on her profile for the world to see. Or was it just for me? As I jealously suspected, I had been both physically and virtually replaced.

Fury saw her one last time. She had a margarita to go from El Sombrero, the Mexican restaurant I showed her on Ludlow Street. He was directing his third student film at Beacon High School, and at sixteen, was also babysitting. She laughed when he told her he got paid eight dollars an hour.

"That's not even cab fare," she scoffed with pompous glee.

"Well, thanks for all the ones you paid for, bitch," Fury said and walked away.

I thought Winky and I had had a real bond, believing despite the difference in our age and status that we had a connection. I was the daddy who was always around, and she was the mom who supported me. I had imagined we would become famous together, eventually becoming lovers when she came of age. Now, she had done the mature thing and moved on, while I felt emotionally fourteen again—hurt, alone, and lost. I signed onto Myspace where it had all started, went to her page, and left one last comment: "You're fat." I was enraged to read her misspelled response the next day: "fuckin alkoholik, take down Royal Young, the name is nothing without me."

13
Dead Meat

"We're closed for a private party," snipped the tall event coordinator in a shiny lavender gown at Stella McCartney store in the Meatpacking District.

"I'm with MQ Publications," I said and shot her a haughty look.

The only thing easing my hurt from Winky's dismissal was throwing myself into a star-studded night out, possibly my last before Dad disowned me. The cream-colored store filled with mirrors and designer dresses was a lavish Band-Aid. Fuck my curfew. I felt like being surrounded by famous faces who would put me together again.

A perk of working for the British-based publisher of coffee-table books was their hot new release, *The R. Crumb Handbook*. The acid-fried perverted comic artist from the '60s with a penchant for *zaftig* women was in town to promote his latest tome. His curly-haired wife, Aline, had been kicking up one leg and touching her ankle to her forehead, like a nympho aerobics instructor all over the office for the past week. Stella McCartney had gotten wind of the *Handbook* and decided to make a line of limited R. Crumb illustrated T-shirts and throw a party complete with his favorite music performed by a swing band.

My ex-babysitter boss took me around like I was still her ward.

"This is my assistant, Hazak," she introduced me.

"I prefer Royal," I corrected her, embarrassed.

"Shut up, that's stupid," she scolded.

I guzzled vodka martinis and tried to catch the attention of socialite

Patrick McMullan's party photographers. Having planned for one last highly publicized hurrah before my parents lost patience with me, I looked like a weird pimp in tight black jeans, a real white-mink vest, and gold chains. Without Winky on my elbow, I again resorted to outrageous costumes to grab attention. Outside, I was outré, but inside she'd taken an irreplaceable piece of me.

As I posed for photos, I imagined Winky seeing my snapshot in the society pages and wanting me back. I noticed a fat bearded man in pink sunglasses and a fuchsia rhinestone cowboy hat glaring at me, but I kept trying to look camera-ready. I was laughing and dancing when excited whispers began rippling through the crowd. The area by the door was cleared and a tiny woman entered in an all-white suit and black shades flanked by massive bodyguards: Yoko Ono.

A lightning storm of flashbulbs started snapping. I pushed people out of the way to get closer. As I elbowed past the rhinestone cowboy, he shoved me hard, making me spill my drink down my pants so it looked like I'd pissed myself.

"Wearing fur to a Stella McCartney store? Get the fuck out of here," he hissed.

"Fuck you," I shot back.

"Who was that?" I asked our PR girl who was doubled over laughing.

"Jay McCarroll. He just won the first season of *Project Runway*. Didn't you know Stella is a hardcore vegan and PETA supporter?"

"I had no clue," I admitted, watching as Jay McCarroll lifted up his poncho, stuck two full champagne flutes underneath, and marched out of the party.

"Did you miss the bathroom?" my boss asked, arching her perfectly plucked eyebrows as she sidled up to me.

"Drink spilled," I said lamely, reaching for two more.

By the time my pants dried I was chatting with my CEO's stylish daughter and feeling famous. My mink vest was getting so much attention I half wished Stella would show up and throw me out of the store herself. It would put me in the Page Six headlines. Crumb's daughter's boyfriend ripped off his shirt and staggered around smoking a cigarette, screaming, "Shitheads!" Guests pretended not to notice, as security carried him off. I watched, half-envious and half-depressed. A nobody had nabbed the spotlight, but it was him, not me.

A pretty girl nearby started laughing. "I'm guessing acid or shrooms," she said. "He must be tripping balls." The party was dying down, but I was pumped with adrenaline, wanting to milk my high for all it was worth. I looked important enough to be persuasive, and a hot girl on my shoulder would help me feel wanted again after the stupid way I'd fallen for Winky.

"Do you want to go to another party?" I asked her.

"I have a photo shoot at eight in the morning for a hair commercial," she said, giving me a sexy smile, like she wanted to blow it off.

"You're coming with me," I boldly took her hand, wandering over to say goodnight to my employer.

"Here's money for a cab, Hazak," garbled my wasted ex-babysitter boss, wobbling on her Manolos and shoving three twenty-dollar bills into my hands. "If anything happens to you, your parents will have my head."

"It's Royal and you're drunk," I told her.

"Remember, Mr. Royal, you better show up at the office tomorrow," she slurred.

The hair model and I tripped happily off into the night and I felt like king of the Meatpacking District. While I was trying to figure out where we should go next on the corner of 10th Avenue and 14th Street, a hulking black-clad figure in a dark top hat scurried past us.

"That was Boy George," said the hair model, turning to me, her blue eyes wide with excitement.

"No way."

"I swear. Don't let him get away." She grabbed my hand like it was a ticket and we followed the man into a club blasting '80s hits.

"Name?" said a bouncer, halting us with one beefy hand, while parting a velvet rope for the mystery man.

"I'm with MQ Publications," I said, emboldened by vodka and wanting to impress my date.

The bouncer scowled and looked at his list.

"Nope," he declared, pushing me aside to let in the couple in line behind us, who were with *Vanity Fair*.

"I have an idea," I whispered in the hair model's ear.

We ducked down in the crowd and swerved past the bouncer in a crush of people.

"Look, there he is!" She pointed as we sat at a table filled with vodka and mixers in cut-glass decanters. I pretended not to remember one of the hostesses I recognized from LaGuardia high school. We had both been told at assemblies that we'd be legends, but she was a waitress and I was a desperate crasher in the playpen of the elite.

Across the room I spotted the black-hatted stranger talking with infamous transvestite Amanda Lepore, whose collagen-infused lips looked like a Mrs. Potato Head accessory. Amanda must have noticed my concentrated scrutiny because she tapped her companion on the shoulder, and Boy George turned around, staring back at me through the crowd, smiling and winking. Then he smooched Amanda Lepore's cheek and vanished past the bouncer into the night.

"Whoa! Did you see that?" The hair model looked on in awe.

Instead of being excited, the attention left me feeling empty and secretly yearning for a loving family and Winky's adolescent kisses.

"Let's go downtown. Do you have cash?" asked the hair model.

"Of course," I smiled, as I hailed down a cab. I felt like I had switched roles with Winky. Now I was the one who had money and could sneak into luxury parties jam-packed with celebrities. I understood the power Winky must have felt she had over me, how quickly people bowed down to status, even when it was being faked. The girl in the taxi was caught up in my act, and so was I. For the first time in a while I felt like I had control over my life—that I could do anything.

We pulled up to Dark Room on the corner of Ludlow and Houston. The streets of the Lower East Side were packed with hipsters in suede boots and rich kids looking for a seedy thrill. I paid for the cab, spilled out, and sauntered up to the bouncer.

"I.D.?" he asked.

"I'm with—" I started.

"I.D.?" he repeated.

"How old are you?" the hair model asked.

"Twenty," I whispered to her. "You can go ahead if you want to—I should head home anyway."

"Are you sure?" she asked as the bouncer let in a string of underage kids decked out in shiny pastel American Apparel leggings.

I wasn't even sure I could safely call my parents' house my "home." My night had come crashing down—too young to get into the hip clubs in my own neighborhood, too old to live in my childhood apartment. I could try to escape into fame and glamorous parties as much as I wanted, but Winky was right, I was still a downtown derelict named Hazak.

I watched the hair model slip happily into Dark Room, without looking back now that I was baggage. I stumbled away feeling inadequate. I headed towards Lucien on First and Houston, a French bistro where my friend Mary bartended. Even though everything else in my life was uncertain, I could always get a free drink there.

"Hey, it's my favorite drunkard," grinned Mary, pale-skinned with a black pixie cut and one flashy gold-grill capped tooth.

I sat at a back table and she slammed down a full bottle of Glenfiddich scotch. The restaurant's walls were a pleasant ochre. In the candlelight, surrounded by polite chatter, I could forget my fear of going home to a psychological war zone.

When I came to, I was in Mary's cramped apartment on Third Street and First Avenue with a giant coffee mug full of whiskey. There were lines of coke laid out on a mirror in front of me, and I was talking incoherently about Winky and being famous.

"I really loved her. I know she was just fourteen, but she was so innocent and lonely like me. Maybe if I make it she'll want me back. She'll be legal in four years so we can have sex and get married. She was my muse after Georgie dumped me and decided she was a lesbian again."

It was four in the morning. As we smoked a joint to calm down and watched David Lynch's *Wild At Heart*, the violent love in the movie started me thinking about Georgie. She seemed like one of the few clean spots in my life before the now unattainable Winky.

"I need to go to someone," I said, as I waved to Mary, staggering down her narrow stairs and out the front door into blinding early morning light.

"It's me," I slurred when Georgie picked up her phone, "Can I see you?"

"I'm getting ready to leave for work. Meet me on my stoop in ten minutes," she said quickly, distracted and confused.

"I miss you," I said and hung up, then tripped through Tompkins Square Park toward her building like a sleepwalker. It was cold, but bright. The last of autumn's leaves hung ragged from the park trees, clinging, like the drunks on the benches, to the last bit of warm hospitality. I had no idea what I wanted to tell Georgie, but I was alone and needed to see a friendly face. Chasing after connections to celebrity meant that most of my ties with old friends had been severed. I was always rushing ahead, greedy for the future, clawing madly toward anything that seemed like it could lift me out of myself. I knew a lot of strangers in passing, but felt Georgie was the only one I had really shared my fantasies and body with. I hadn't had a real, consuming, or responsible romantic relationship in almost six years.

When I got to Georgie's stoop there was no sign of her. High on coke, weed, and whiskey, I waited, paranoid. Every second, I imagined Georgie was upstairs finishing breakfast with her new female lover— laughing, sober, secure. She'd probably think I was disgusting, reeking of last night's debauchery. I was a pathetic boy from her past, on a pointless search for any comforting presence.

I started walking away as fast as I could, passing quickly through Alphabet City and into the Lower East Side. Even Avenue B had been overrun by bistros and sidewalk cafes where people dined luxuriously yet simply, sipping and supping with no sense for the history of the streets around them. But every corner was covered in ghosts for me: the garden with crooked ivy wrapped 'round the iron fence; the statue of towering toys and found objects reaching tremulously into the sky; the bodegas that were still left; the stoops where I had spilled beer, skinned knees, held hands. The world around me was a million pieces of the past, all crying, curious, and crowded together, and no one could hear or see them but me.

Luckily, my parents weren't awake when I got home and the chain lock was off. I snuck into my room, feeling unwanted, and passed out on my bed in all my clothes, white mink sticking to my cheek.

When I woke up at noon, I ran past my parents, who were cooking omelets. The smell of frying eggs and cheese made me feel sick as I slammed the bathroom door. I turned on the hot water in the shower full blast and crouched underneath the spray on the tile floor, vomiting uncontrollably.

＊

"We need to talk," Dad said.

He and Mom were sitting on the orange couch in the living room, surrounded by African masks and the artwork they had collected from thrift shops as I grew up, which had not changed much since I was a child. I shivered, dripping wet in my bathrobe. My hands were shaking and my stomach rumbled from my night of bingeing. I tried to smile. Since they'd gotten me a job, my relationship with my parents wasn't as tortured, but the stern look on Dad's face and the resigned one on Mom's made me nervous.

"You living here just isn't working," my father said bluntly.

I looked to Mom.

"It's for the best," she said and tried to smile, looking away. "You're out all hours of the night doing god knows what, getting stoned. You're not in school and are disrespectful to your father and to me."

"Are those your reasons or are you just regurgitating Dad's, like always?"

"Your father and I share a lot of opinions. Why don't we go out for a nice lunch?" Mom suggested.

"No. I'm sick of food instead of answers. I'm only twenty years old. Sorry if I'm still trying to figure out how to live my life," I said.

"You have two weeks," my father replied. "I want you out of my house."

14
Ghetto Superstar

The next week, I started throwing all my outrageous Manhattan outfits into giant heavy-duty Hefty bags. Cecelia, my high-school lover, was frantically looking for a roommate after the heroin-addicted girl she lived with left for Egypt owing $2,000 in back rent. Even though Cecelia lived in a dimly lit railroad apartment in Bushwick, a bad Brooklyn neighborhood, I hoped being in close quarters with the girl who had first broken my heart would heal whatever was left of it. I was even happy to trash the tight jeans, glittering tops, fringe suede vests, and fur coats I'd donned in a desperate bid for downtown acclaim. I knew I'd get beaten and robbed if I ran around the ghetto looking like a wannabe glam-rocker.

"See, you spent so much money on this shit and now it's worthless," Dad said, passing me as I packed the cheap, flashy vintage things I'd spent my publishing money on. They didn't even cost much.

I ignored him. Mom and Dad refused to help me move, so I had enlisted the help of Babbi, my grandmother. Though I had kept her nurturing presence out of my life, afraid she'd pinpoint me as a *nogoodnik* right away, she seemed pleased to drive my few possessions over the Williamsburg Bridge in defiance of Dad, her son-in-law.

"Your father is a sad, angry man," she commiserated, as her car touched down on the Brooklyn side. "Pathetic, making his own son live in such a bad neighborhood. He certainly believes in suffering." She shook her head.

"He hates me now," I said.

"And what about your mother?" Babbi continued. "I didn't raise her to act this way. Listening to whatever that man says. She needs to stand up for her children. But ever since she was little, she couldn't handle a conflict. Life is a conflict. You have to fight for what you want in this world."

"I'll never stop fighting," I reassured her.

"I'm here to help you no matter what. But you should think about going back to college." Babbi patted my knee with her gnarled hand as cold rain fell outside the car windows on a grey city. Somewhere in the distance of my new neighborhood a car horn honked out *The Godfather* theme.

The next day, when I was back at my parents' to grab my stash of *High Society* porn magazines from under my old bed, Cecelia called their house phone.

"So, new roomie, I was like totally sleeping when I woke up and your grandmother was in my room just standing over me and staring."

"What?" I laughed.

Their old rotary phone was still in the dining room and Mom and Dad looked up at me suspiciously.

"Yeah. This creepy old lady was hovering over me and when I opened my eyes she handed me a cell phone and said it was for you. She said the door was unlocked."

"I'm so sorry. Babbi would never hurt you," I said.

"What's going on?" Dad demanded when I hung up. As if that old and horrible phone intervention with Cecelia was replaying itself.

"Oh, Babbi just broke into my apartment to give me a cell," I said and smiled at Mom. "You know how she is."

"That controlling bitch!" Dad exploded. "You don't need anything she has to give you. I hate mobile phones. How dare she just waltz into your personal space!"

"Well, I do sort of need it to call my friends and you," I pointed out.

But Dad wasn't listening as he grabbed the phone out of my hands and started furiously dialing. "I want you to stay away from my son. I don't give a fuck what you think. This is my kid and I set the rules for him," Dad screamed.

I didn't wait to hear the rest, slamming my parents' door. I ran blindly through Sarah Delano Roosevelt Park, collapsing on a bench near the subway, sobbing hot, angry tears.

%&$#?@!

I tried to avoid Manhattan as much as I could after that. I e-mailed my resignation to my publishing boss. In some ways, it was a relief to put the city behind me, to sink completely into a simple diet of Tropical Fantasy soda and Honey BBQ potato chips. The pursuit of fame, the pressure of attempting to annihilate any remnants of the sweet and sad little boy I had been, had wasted my body. Bones jutted through my thinness, sagging flesh hung where muscle should have been. My grey eyes had developed a floating quality, as if always struggling to rise to the top of a puddle of lethally alcoholic punch. I felt defeated, demoralized, and had stopped caring.

I wandered the streets of Bushwick, reminded of the lost Lower East Side of my youth. The only tall, thin rail of a white kid on the blocks around my new apartment, I stalked past broken forty-ounce bottles, basketball hoops nailed to streetlights, weeds pushing through cracks in sidewalks, hydrants freed of water, flooding gutters, rats ta-thump, ta-thumping through the garbage cans and scurrying from the orange circles of streetlamp light when dusk descended.

Cecelia and I hit blunts, leaning out the cracked windows of her top-floor bedroom, the sky blue above old, low buildings—not high like in the city. In these brief moments, I felt my world was open. While my lungs filled, my heart boomed fast and close to breaking.

I practiced the broken Spanish I'd picked up from Mom at my new corner bodega in Bushwick. Coming back with a forty-ounce of Colt 45 and a bag of Cheetos, my Babbi phone started ringing. Winky was on the caller ID.

"Your very surly little brother told me you moved to Brooklyn, love," she purred in her English accent when I picked up.

"Yes, I'm stuck in the ghetto," I admitted.

"Don't worry. I'm hopping in a cab to save you. I need a date," Winky giggled.

Cecelia was staying over in the city. It would be a perfect night to seduce Winky and win her back. Then I could at least sleep on the Upper East Side for a night. I was still twenty, but Winky had turned fifteen and her casual confidence always made her seem older.

Winky's taxi got lost and I had to pick her up five blocks away from my apartment. She was wearing an oversized brown fur coat and looking scared. Her black hair was curled flirtatiously around her face and her eyes were heavy with makeup. She shivered in front of the dilapidated mansions on Bushwick Avenue. I felt a protective rush come over me when I saw her. I missed her. I was thrilled that apparently she'd dumped me only temporarily.

"I'm so sorry I called you fat. I always thought you were beautiful," I told her.

"You're still Royal to me, darling," she moaned as I hugged her. "Where are we?"

"The hood," I said anxiously, putting my arm over her shoulder and steering her back toward the semi-safety of my building. Winky's panicky face and luxurious fur gave us away as an easy target in the wrong neighborhood. Winky took one look at my decrepit apartment filled with empty beer bottles and overflowing ashtrays and whipped out her cell phone.

"Baby, we're calling another cab and getting out of here," she announced.

"No rush," I said, leading her into my graffittied bedroom.

I put on 50 Cent's "The Massacre." The heavy bass beats made my thin walls shake as he rapped about his crack-addicted baby mama who needed him for another hit.

I didn't care about our ages anymore. Her rich-girl-in-the-ghetto predicament turned me on. We started making out and I pressed against her so she could feel me hard. She got on her tiptoes as I ran my hands under her shirt. Then she pushed me away.

"We should go to the party," she said.

"But I want you. I'm ready for you," I said.

"Do you have a phone number for a car service?" she asked, taking out her cell phone again and walking into the kitchen.

We rolled off the Williamsburg Bridge on the Manhattan side of the river. My parents' block rushed past outside the windows. Winky and I held hands and kissed.

"Did you miss me?" she asked.

"You know I did," I said, burying my face in her fur coat and inhaling her Chanel perfume.

I wished I never had to go back to Brooklyn, that she would sweep me away into her opulent life. Yet now that I'd traded bohemian chic on Eldridge Street for exile in my Bushwick crack den, I feared I'd lost my appeal to her. Without a sugar mommy to speed me off in taxi chariots, I might be permanently stuck in the ghetto.

When we got to the party at a townhouse on the Upper East Side, I realized why Winky had brought me. I was the only guy in a gaggle of sex-starved, underage rich girls who were having a pajama and champagne soiree in a fifteen-year-old Juicy Couture heiress's massive penthouse. I wasn't Winky's date, I was everyone's—just another of her throwaway playthings. I popped bottles of Moet and insisted on recording "Row Your Boat" in harmony with Winky on Juicy's sleek Mac laptop.

"Can I kiss him?" Juicy asked Winky. "He's so cute."

"I'll take pictures," Winky giggled, grabbing Juicy's digital camera.

I made out with Juicy while the other girls cheered.

At 2 a.m. Winky dropped me off in a cab by Union Square, so I could take the L train home. We stood on the corner by the boarded up Virgin megastore, where we had first met.

"This is as far as I go," she said.

"Will you visit me again?" I asked.

"Daddy's moving us to London, love," she said and hugged me. "I'll write you."

I broke away before she could continue and stumbled into the subway.

My first week adjusting to Winky's permanent good bye, Cecelia and I walked all over Bushwick, scouting out cheap thrift shops under the rumbling elevated train tracks and staring greedily at plush, powder blue leather couches in a big discount department store called Fat Albert's. Cecelia had gone from the girl I lost my virginity to in high school to an old friend in need of a roommate. I had memories of Cecelia's mom as an abusive matriarch who had accused me of raping her daughter. Yet despite this, and my father manipulating Cecelia into calling child services on her, her mother sent me care packages of homemade mashed potatoes with Swedish meatballs and cans of Arizona Iced Tea.

"She feels bad about how things are with your dad," Cecelia explained. "She knows parents can be rough on their kids."

I savored her mother's meals when I woke up hung over and broke, imagining my father had sent me Tupperware containers of his special lemon chicken. One night when I had finished eating, I got so drunk I blacked out and woke up with a black eye. It was impossible to remember how I'd gotten it.

The next day, I ventured back to my childhood home for the first time since my latest fight with my father, planning it so that Dad would be at work teaching ceramics to blind people. I had no money and hadn't eaten all day. Mom buzzed me in. She was alone and packed a bag for me full of Bumblebee tuna, Progresso Chicken Soup and bialys.

"Is your neighborhood okay?" she asked, furtively adding Granny Smith apples. "What happened to your eye?"

"It's fine, Mom. Thanks for the food." I hugged her good-bye.

"I love you." Mom's voice broke, like she wanted to say more, but was too much under Dad's control. I was grateful, but felt like a stranger in their house. Even if I told Mom the truth about my life, she would always take Dad's side. I couldn't have gone back again, even if I wanted to.

%&$#?@!

"I know it's sort of hood here, but when we were growing up, Manhattan wasn't so safe either. If we stick together, we'll be fine," Cecelia assured me.

She was another lost white kid thrown into a neighborhood where she—and I—stuck out. She was obsessed with celebrity gossip rags like *Star, OK!* and *InTouch* magazine. She left them strewn around the apartment. Right away the glossy covers crammed with scandals caught my eye. I couldn't help but notice that the crack house down the block, with its boarded-up windows and steady stream of toothless inhabitants, was a stark contrast to the headlines glorifying luxury vacations in Cabo San Lucas and the paparazzi pictures of the best beach bodies. The celebrities caught in the paparazzi's lens became a kind of faraway "fame" family, now that I was without my real one. I also noticed the tide of American culture turning.

Though there was still a widespread obsession with celebrity, it seemed as the cracks in my life grew wider, so did the reportage of celebrity breakdowns. Paris Hilton, the princess of being famous for doing nothing, so long a figure America had been fascinated with—a blonde blank slate onto which the country's dreams had been projected—was going to jail. Images of her crumpled, crying face seen through a squad car window were everywhere. It seemed my country punished celebrity as much as they elevated it, building celluloid gods of mythic proportions only to tear them down.

%&$#?@!

Cecelia was a big pothead, but all her old connections lived around gentrified Stuyvesant Town. They didn't want to trek to a dangerous neighborhood to sell a twenty bag. I was also hungry for drugs, coping with the streets around me the same way my father's old clients had. We needed to make fresh narcotive connections in our new neighborhood.

"Just walk up, shake your tits a little, and ask," I said, shoving Cecelia toward a group of teens hanging out on the stoop opposite ours.

"Can't you do it?" She stalled.

"They'd beat me up. You're sexy," I coaxed her, desperate to get high.

I watched as Cecelia giggled and flirted with a tall boy who still had some baby fat. They exchanged a handshake and she rushed back excitedly with a big bag of weed.

"It was only ten dollars," she cried.

"They like your curves," I laughed.

Because of Cecelia's block reputation as "hot white girl with the bubble butt," we became fast friends with Chubbs, a pudgy nineteen-year-old drug dealer. We invited Chubbs to come up to our place and burn a blunt with us. As we smoked I put on my Mobb Deep *The Infamous* record. It was what I heard on the streets growing up. Moving back to the 'hood had given me renewed appreciation for its rugged poetry, and I doubted that Chubbs wanted to listen to Cecelia's Hanson CDs.

"You like this music?" Chubbs asked me incredulously.

"I've had this album since eighth grade," I told him.

"Word." Chubbs looked more comfortable and eased back into our couch. "Yo, I'm mad nervous son," he continued, as he giggled and hit the blunt. "I owe this kid two hundred and fifty dollars."

"Lame," said Cecelia.

"It's aight'. I just bought a Benz." Chubbs burst out laughing.

Chubbs had grown up on the block and everyone knew him. He lived with his mom across the street, but was otherwise secretive about his life. Sometimes when he was stoned he'd reminisce about the one time he had visited the Dominican Republic.

"We slept outside by the beach, yo. It was mad dark, no electricity, nothing. I could only hear the water."

He was a street celebrity who looked out for us. Within weeks I was downing forty-ounce bottles of Colt 45 and slurring in Spanish to the middle-aged woman at my corner bodega. She winked at me and sold me bootleg packs of Marlboro Reds for $5.00 with a green *Republica Dominica* stamp on the side. Chubbs' limelight spread to Cecelia and me and I felt so safe I let down my guard and found myself having fun. The block was even more exciting than the elite New York City circuit I had been booted from. The risks seemed real, with higher-up drug dealers giving orders, and the appearance of spotlights, like at a movie premiere, but from police helicopters.

Cecelia and I spent lazy days smoking weed and doing photo shoots with her cheap digital camera. In pursuit of better location shots, we climbed through the narrow hatchway in the ceiling to the roof. Once, Cecelia found an empty 9mm clip on the silver, spray-painted tarmac on top of our building.

"I should make it into a necklace," she said, tucking it in her pocket.

"That's it, I'm getting ya'll a gun," Chubbs announced, when she showed it to him later.

"What? We'd get drunk and shoot each other," I blurted.

Cecelia and I stared at him. We looked at each other and burst out laughing.

"This isn't funny. You need protection." Chubbs looked at us like we were crazy.

I couldn't stop laughing and neither could Cecelia. We doubled up—holding onto each other so we wouldn't fall down.

To make extra money I took the Long Island Rail Road out to Great Neck on weekends, so I could mow the lawn for my grandparents. Their three-story house, surrounded by fir trees and a sloping garden, was an escape from the crooked, cracked asphalt of Brooklyn.

"You need some nice clothes. They'll be your ticket out," Babbi said, slipping me five twenties and a plastic Costco bag full of kugel and strawberries.

"It's good to come up here and get some fresh air," Zayde said. "Here, pour a siplet in your cuplet," he added, spilling out generous gin and tonics for the three of us as a prelude to big steak dinners later that night.

"I mean, your father doesn't even eat red meat. Silly man," Babbi said as she heaped onions over my steaming slice of Angus beef. Without my parents' love, my grandparents were the only family I had, except for my brother. Even though I spent most of the money they gave me on more liquor, their encouragement seeped through my guarded suspicion of anyone who wanted to love me.

When I had time to myself, I secretly scribbled in my tattered composition books, working on my novel about a son in an incestuous relationship with his insane mother who returns to their gothic mansion to murder her. I hoped I could send the rough pages to Greg, the agent at Wilhelmina. Even though he specialized in fashion I was sure he knew every important person in the city. One of them had to help me. If I sold it I could afford to move back to Manhattan and prove to Dad I was writing the "great American novel" he insisted I would never pen.

I often didn't have enough money for subway fare and walked over the Williamsburg Bridge to my parents' house. I tried to avoid my angry Dad and apologetic Mom to see Fury. We shared a bottle of wine on the building's roof garden, looking out over lower Manhattan.

"Do you have a short story I could adapt into a movie?" Fury asked one day. "I want to make something good for my final project this year."

He was taking a digital film class, which engaged him entirely. Spending the weekends with me in Bushwick, drinking himself into oblivion, along with an acute teenage temper, had resulted in Fury's wanting to drop out of high school. But the film class he was taking was finally allowing him to pursue the dreams he'd had since childhood.

"I've been thinking a lot about different events happening at once along a psychic time/space continuum," I rambled. "A kidnapped girl, an aging alcoholic, a man on the run, and a Wall Street broker jerking off. We could call it $e = mc^2$. And have a big red carpet premiere," I said, daydreaming.

"We'll paper the whole city with posters," he promised.

As my brother put his key in our parents' door, Dad quickly opened it. Our father's angry gaze scrutinized me immediately. I was holding an empty bottle of cheap cabernet and two coffee mugs. His eyes took on the same roiling, animal rage I had seen as a child when he hit my dog.

"Were you drinking?" he yelled, grabbing my brother by the collar of his shirt and yanking him inside.

"It was just me. He didn't have any," I lied.

"Get the fuck off me," Fury said, shoving Dad against the wall.

"You son of a bitch!" Dad screamed, raising his hand to hit Fury.

"Stop!" I got in between them.

"You're turning the smartest person in this family into a drunk like you. You have your own place in Brooklyn. Stay there," Dad snapped in my face.

"I'm trying to be friends with my little brother. I'm trying to be mature. Maybe you should grow the fuck up and try to be a father," I yelled back.

"Get out!" Dad's face was white. "Stay out."

%&$#?@!

Chubbs started coming over more frequently. He never touched cocaine, but he had good, cheap $20 grams, and he always got Cecelia and me stoned, sometimes letting us sample his blow too.

"Olsen girl, Lindsay Lohan, all those bitches sniff like crazy 'cause they just don't care. They got everything," Chubbs philosophized.

I wasn't sure I agreed, but that didn't stop me from snorting thick lines through milk shake straws from McDonald's whenever I had the chance. Chubbs thought we were rich because we were white; no amount of explaining could convince him otherwise. For extra money I sold coke for him, but I lasted only a week. I wound up snorting my stash and then having to pay $100 for it.

I shaved my head and put lines through my eyebrows, so I looked more like a ghetto superstar. I stalked Winky, Georgie, and Greg on Myspace. Judging from the Internet, it seemed as if they were leading busy, successful lives in Manhattan. Winky and Harry Potter Boy were still leaving love-struck comments; Georgie posted pictures of her making out with indie girl; and Greg had stopped responding to my messages in favor of posting photos of himself traveling the world. I drank 40s on my stoop with Chubbs and his friends. Chubbs would also come over to the apartment, and I'd help him weigh and bag ounces of dry weed into Ziploc bags with Scooby Doo printed on them. I felt cut off from everyone, but at least I was a part of something.

I decided to throw myself a party to celebrate turning twenty-one at my new apartment and made up a long guest list, including Winky and all her rich friends. Doing bumps of blow, I chewed compulsively on my pen, scratching names in my black-and-white composition notebook. Finally legal drinking age, I couldn't afford to go out to any bars and was desperate for a taste of luxury, even if it was from a pampered fifteen-year-old who'd dumped me. On the night of the party no one showed. I knew it was because they were scared to cross Winky, not to mention the Williamsburg Bridge. She never called. Fury, always there for me, came over and we ended up blasting G-Unit and getting wasted off a handle of cheap rum called Boca Chica.

"I can't believe no one showed up," I said.

"I'm here," he reminded me.

"Winky isn't," I said.

"She's in high school. She won't help you out of this. You need to do it yourself," Fury said.

I woke up at 5 p.m. the next night and saw blue flashlight beams circling around my darkened living room through my open bedroom door. I lay frozen on my bed, closed my eyes, and prayed "they" would leave without killing me. When I opened my eyes the flashlights were still there. I saw the bulky shapes of two men. I was being robbed. I lay still, pretending to sleep and listening to them stumbling around clumsily. Finally I heard the intruders leave and the apartment go quiet. I got up, turned on all the lights, and discovered the bathroom window had been forced. Razors, soap, and shampoo had been knocked into the tub. Our computer was gone, but the mouse was still there, its cord leading nowhere.

15
Delusions of Grandeur

"They used to dump corpses on Crosby Street when I first moved to New York from Chicago in the '60s, but I never got robbed," Dad commiserated. "You know what, Hazak? You're tough."

Sitting safe in my parents' living room, I smiled at the hint of approval.

"At least you didn't get hurt, God forbid. That's what counts," Mom said, hugging me.

Cecelia decided to crash at her mother's in Manhattan for a night, while black metal bars were put over our bathroom window in Bushwick.

For the first time since I had left for Bennington Mom and Dad showed concern about my well-being. Fury had taken over my old room, but sleeping on my parent's couch, with sheets that smelled like Tide detergent instead of cigarette smoke, made me feel like a child again. When I woke up, sun poured through the windows, and Mom was making breakfast.

"Good morning, sweetie. Do you want some coffee?" she asked.

"That would be amazing, thanks." I felt grateful and comforted by her presence. It was nicer than not having money to eat and being greeted by Cecelia's dirty cereal bowls.

"I went to Gourmet Garage in SoHo and bought all your favorite foods. Prosciutto, strawberries, and croissants for breakfast." Mom and I exchanged smiles as I sat down with her at our dining room table. I was happy we were getting along, but still scared. At twenty-one, getting fed by Mom soothed me. Yet, I feared my father would be livid if he came up from his studio and caught her spoiling me.

After breakfast, I quickly called Cecelia to see if Brooklyn could be an escape hatch from my father's wrath.

"I spoke to my mom and it's official, baby, I'm going to Amsterdam!" Cecelia screamed.

"You're moving to Holland?" I asked.

"No, silly. My cousin Judy and I are going on vacation. I cannot deal with the ghetto right now."

I couldn't believe her formerly abusive mother had mended their relationship, while I had lost my parents' love. I wondered if she'd morph into jet-setting Winky, flying off to glamorous destinations and leaving me. The thought of living in Bushwick without her made me ache. I imagined the burglars returning to kill me before I was famous or could fix my relationship with my family. I didn't want to test my parents' sudden and comforting Jewish hospitality by asking them to let me stay with them for longer than one night.

"We need to talk," I said as I sat Mom and Dad down in their living room where we always had family discussions. I had asked Fury to be there too for back-up. I wanted to tell our parents how isolated and lost I felt in Bushwick and ask for their help finding another apartment in a less sketchy part of the borough.

"I'm so glad you agree about opening up channels of discussion," Dad commented.

"We've seen a therapist who thinks we should all go in for counseling," Mom said.

Fury and I exchanged pained looks. We had to communicate in code in front of shrink parents who overanalyzed every word. They could fix their client's problems, but the damage in our own family was beyond diagnosis. We needed outside analysis.

"Let's try," I shrugged.

"Whatever," Fury said.

"Great. We'll set up an appointment with Dr. Craig next week. His office is in Midwood. You can meet us in the city and we'll all go out together," Dad said.

I didn't understand why we had to take the Q train so far into Brooklyn for an hour session once a week. Midwood is in the center of Brooklyn—a long ride—and Mom knew plenty of therapists in Manhattan.

"Who recommended Dr. Craig again?" I asked my father skeptically as we swayed on the rumbling subway.

"His prices, very cheap," Dad said.

"Everything you do has to be cheap," Fury complained.

"Then you foot the bills," Dad said, jabbing his finger into Fury's chest.

The neighborhood was filled with Hasidic Jews and old women whose heads were wrapped in faded brown babushkas. Dr. Craig's office was on the first floor of an unlived-in apartment building. He had a small, cramped waiting room, with dated, tattered copies of *People* magazine on a tiny coffee-table. I mentally compared it to Mom's waiting room, which was spacious, with lime green walls, filled with Moroccan prints and framed artwork that I had painted in high school.

"Welcome," Dr. Craig said as he opened the door to his office.

"This is Hazak, aka Royal, and this is Yuvi, aka Fury, our two big problems." My father introduced my brother and me before we even sat down.

"I like Royal and Fury. What do they mean?" Dr. Craig inquired.

"They just look so much better in movie credits," Fury explained.

"A girl I loved gave me mine," I said, omitting Winky's age.

"Bullshit! Who do you think brought you into this world? Who do you think changed your diapers? You know we were going to call you *Shtarky*, it means strong in Yiddish, but we thought 'the kid will hate us with a name like that.' You got lucky," my father said.

"You used to sign paintings under a pseudonym, and you had your name legally changed," I reminded him.

"So did we," Fury said.

"Do you hate being Jewish?" Mom wrung her hands.

"I love that I'm Jewish, Mom, but being named Hazak was like walking around wrapped in a giant Israeli flag," I said.

"Why are we here?" Dr. Craig winced as though he was afraid to get hit. He was a tall sheepish man with thick black eyebrows.

"They made us come," Fury grumbled.

"We've been in a rut for months. Communication has broken down completely," Dad interjected.

"Are you delusional? Months? How about forever?" I said.

"We're the perfect parents—kind, compassionate, permissive." Dad ticked off their good qualities on his fingers.

"Inappropriate, stingy, shitheads."

I counted on mine, staring at Dad.

"It's not nice to mimic your father," Mom said, shifting in her seat next to Dad and looking uncomfortable. Dr. Craig sat back. I wondered if he was going to jump in and mediate, but he just rubbed his hands together and looked thoughtful.

"You're the one that's a negative influence on your little brother, getting drunk all the time." Dad pointed at me.

"I can make my own decisions and I don't want to be here," Fury said.

"I'm worried and confused. I don't understand where all this anger is coming from," Mom put in.

"Well, that's what we're here to find out, isn't it?" Dad retorted. "You sit there worried and confused while your two sons are screwing up left and right, but you never get angry. You just let it go on."

"Why do you let Dad bully you?" I asked her.

Mom gave Dad a wounded look. Fury laughed.

"What's so funny? You're not exactly innocent, mister Yuvele," Dad pointed at him. "Doing swastika graffiti in school is setting yourself up for failure."

"Wait. Fury graffittied a swastika in school?" Dr. Craig asked.

"I told you. We raised them to be sensitive, nice Jewish boys, and my own son is anti-Semitic. And where is Hazak in all this? He's your little brother, he looks up to you. How could you let him do this?" Mom turned to me.

"I told you, I can make my own decisions." Fury shouted. "Why do you have to analyze everything, Mom? I hate school and there was a big poster of smiley faces, I drew some swastikas over. I just wanted to show people the world isn't all happy. Every little action I make is not a huge Freudian dilemma and I'm not a neo-Nazi."

"The kid was just trying to stir things up with art, like me." Dad changed his tone, looking a little pleased.

"I don't care!" Mom's face flushed red. "I hate my own sons," she started to cry.

I felt bitterly proud of Mom for breaking out and admitting her truth. It made the distance between us more bearable. I was starting to see the shape of the angry silences, slammed doors, and sadness that had stalked me in my parents' house.

"Alright, there's definitely negative energy in the room," Dr. Craig said calmly. "Look, I see a lot of families, and from my experience if it's just a shouting match, things are pretty irreparable and there's no point in you coming here. Why don't you all talk and figure out if you want another session?"

I couldn't believe he didn't have any more insightful comments. We couldn't repair the rift in our family if we were going to a bargain-basement shrink.

%&$#?@!

Fury and I walked ahead of our parents through the dark streets of Midwood as I moodily smoked a Marlboro Red. There were well-kept houses on the tree-lined streets, unlike Bushwick, and warm yellow light spilled out of living room windows where I imagined uncomplicated Polish families with happy children were watching TV after pierogi dinners. My stomach rumbled. As usual, I hadn't had enough money to eat all day.

"Are you guys hungry?" Dad shouted at our backs. "There's a famous pizza place by the subway."

Di Faro's pizzeria was packed and the walls were plastered in newspaper clippings bursting with praise. The smell of tomato sauce filled the air. Up until I left for Bennington, my parents had made it a point to have family dinners every night at six sharp, where we all sat down together. Mom and Dad shared case studies without using their patients' names, while my brother and I argued over action heroes. Now, Fury and I were the case studies. We ate pizza in silence and I sipped my Diet Coke.

"This tastes amazing," Dad said, biting into his slice.

"It's really good," Fury agreed.

"I like it too." I found myself smiling.

"So are we going to go back for another session?" Mom asked timidly.

I bit into a piece of fresh basil, the flavor mixing with the mozzarella cheese. "Sure," I said.

I let myself be hopeful on the train ride home. Eating as a family had been more mending than our therapy session. But when I got off in Bushwick, I pulled my hood down over my head, walking quickly over broken bottles as cars blasted bass beats, speeding over bumpy streets. I felt lost again. Mom had admitted she hated us, Dad gloried in the fight, and I was too tired to win back their love. Anger was easier. I recounted mental ammunition so I could get Dr. Craig on my side. I imagined joining Cecelia for amazing adventures in Amsterdam, smoking fat joints in the red light district while sultry hookers beckoned from windows. The empty apartment depressed me and I called Chubbs, asking if he wanted to come over and bag some weed. He did.

I sat on the floor of my bedroom, weighing out greens on his scale, sorting out the stems and seeds. I'd really fallen down the fame food chain to bottom, hanging out with this dodgy drug dealer and his shitty pot. Drinking from a jug of Carlo Rossi with Tony Yayo rapping on my stereo and Chubbs taking phone calls from desperate junkies, I felt hardened enough to not need my parents.

"With Cecelia away, I was thinking I could move into your living room. It would be mad fun. We just ball out every night. You know my mom's has been all on my case lately. She don't like what I do, but I gotta get that money," Chubbs told me.

"I guess everyone has family issues," I mumbled.

"You gotta see this," Chubbs stared at his prepaid Nokia phone.

I knelt next to him and he pressed a button, letting a grainy video roll on the small screen. I could make out him and six other Latino thugs with their baggy pants around their ankles, while a girl in hoop earrings bobbed from dick to dick. They watched her suck off their buddies—vials of crack rock strewn on a table behind them—while loud *bachata* music played.

"Look, dats me," giggled Chubbs.

The view shifted to a close-up of his dark, uncut erection sliding in and out of the girl's mouth, then he came all over her sweatshirt.

"Yo, I got it on her shirt, but I was trying to hit her face," Chubbs laughed.

On his cell phone the girl cursed and the screen went blank. I reached for my glass of cheap wine, hoping to drown out what I had just seen. Watching made me feel dirty, like I was back in a place where sex was a desperate, degrading act.

"If I move in, we'll be pimpin' every night, son," Chubbs offered.

"No thanks," I said.

"But it will be fun." His face fell in disappointment.

"Sorry, dude," I said.

I didn't want to be like him.

%&$#?@!

"Let's start with the artist comments and why money is such a big concern here," Dr. Craig began our second hour-long session. My parents were sitting together again, on his couch, while my brother and I sat across from each other. Two against two.

"He thinks he can be an international celebrity," Dad scoffed, gesturing at me.

"That's not true," I said defensively.

"Then what do you want to do with your life?" he asked.

"Be successful and really well-known in a high-profile job," I replied.

"Let me know how that works out when you're starving on the street," my father guffawed.

"Like you're such a good role model—you don't even have a full-time job," I defended.

"This is the thanks I get?" Dad yelled. "I'm an artist."

"No, you just mooch off Mom's money," I said.

"Part of your father's and my marriage is that I support his art-work," my mother explained.

"So why don't you support your sons?" I asked.

"Oh, so we should just give and give while you run around with these *fakakta* ideas about being famous?" Dad laughed angrily.

"If you were a good parent, yes," I said.

"Is that why you were running around wearing fur coats and lots of gold chains? To get attention?" Mom questioned.

"I don't dress like a freak now that I'm stuck in the ghetto getting robbed," I said.

"Where you put him," Fury added.

"We're thinking of military boot camp for you, you little *pisher*." Dad turned on Fury. "You're self-destructive too."

"I'm making a movie," Fury said.

"He's going to be a director." I stood up for him.

"See how they band together?" Dad appealed.

Dr. Craig nodded noncommittally.

"You're just jealous," I said.

"Yes, I am." Dad surprised me. "Don't you think I have the same underlying grandiosity you do? Where do you think you got it?"

I fell back into my leather chair. I had been presumptuous, think-ing that carrying out our shared fame fantasies would make him proud, not hurt. I loved Dad for sacrificing his dreams for stability and a steady paycheck to feed his kids. Yet he had also always made me feel guilty, as if my birth had marked the end of his museum-show artist myth.

"I feel powerless to help my sons." Mom started to cry.

"Well, I think we're getting somewhere," Dr. Craig said stoically. "Anyone want candy?"

He reached into his desk drawer and took out an arrangement of sugary Airheads.

"We're talking about monitoring these two boys and you're offering them candy?" my father asked.

"It's just some harmless fructose," Dr. Craig protested.

"We need limits and boundaries here," my father lectured him.

"I think you need trust and forgiveness," Dr. Craig said, his hands still holding out the colorfully packaged sweets.

"I'll take a few," Fury said.

"Me too." I grabbed a blue one.

"Do you have any chocolate?" Mom asked.

"Hershey Kisses," Dr. Craig said.

Mom giggled as she bit into the treat. In his own crazy way, I thought Dr. Craig's offer was right. It seemed sustenance was what we had been missing as a family for too long.

Outside in the orange glow of the building's security lights I stood next to my brother, while Dad put his arm around Mom who was wiping at her red eyes with her scarf.

"Are you angry at us?" Dad asked me.

"Yes," I said.

"Well I'm pretty pissed too." He stuck out his tongue at me.

"Why are you mad?"

"Because you are," he said, turning and walking towards the subway.

Throughout the ride Fury and I sat apart from our parents. Even though I wanted to reach out, I still felt like we were strangers. I was trying to be honest about my emotions, but that just seemed to make my father more set against me. As soon as I got off the M train in Bushwick, I made a beeline for the Arab-owned deli to buy more 40s of Colt.

"What up?" Chubbs' voice interrupted my thoughts.

I had been standing in line right next to him and his friend Flaco without noticing. After seeing the sex tape, I had been trying to avoid him. I didn't want to be his roommate and become a white thug superstar anymore. I wanted to move out of the hood and feel closer to my family—though I never admitted that when staring into my parents' angry eyes in therapy.

"This is Curly. You mind if he samples some crack in your crib?" Chubbs pointed to a graying black man missing most of his front teeth and wearing a baggy Northface jacket, fidgeting and grinning behind him.

"No problem," I blurted.

I needed to ignore his request, but my impulsive side wanted a brush with danger.

When the four of us got up to my apartment, I opened my bedroom window, letting in the cool night air. I was curious to see Curly light up a rock, but I didn't want to sleep in crack fumes. Curly whipped out a pipe from the inner recesses of his puffy coat and packed it.

"This is amazing smoke," Chubbs said. "Better than cooked food."

Curly lit up and inhaled, then exploded in a fit of coughing. He smacked his peeling lips, rolling his tongue around his gums like a wine connoisseur.

"Not bad. Pretty good. I'll take ten dollars of that shit," came the high-pitched verdict.

After they left, I noticed some white crack dust on my mirror. I scraped it together, putting a tiny snowcap carefully on top of weed and inhaled it all through my homemade bong. My chest tightened for a few seconds and my vision skipped. I knew Fury was right; I was the only one who could pull myself out of this.

%&$#?@!

Dr. Craig's cramped office in Midwood was the one safety zone I had with a mediator on standby, ready to step in if things got out of hand.

"What about when I called you from Bennington? I was depressed and crying on the floor, and you made it all about you." I confronted Dad in our next session.

"Well, when we were in Maine and I asked you if I seemed alright, you didn't recognize my sadness. You invalidated my feelings," Dad pouted.

"I was thirteen and scared. You told me I had an Oedipal complex right when I started puberty. I never wanted to hurt you, but it seemed like you needed fear and anger between us. It was the only way you could relate to me," I said.

"Look, I had a horrible role model," he responded. "Grandpa Morris was away fighting World War II when I was little. When he wasn't absent, he was scoffing at my artwork. I ran away from him to New York thinking I was going to make it."

"So you know how it feels to want to pursue your passions without your parents' blessing. It's horrible. I need your help. I need to learn from you, not feel like we're in a competition," I said.

"I'm competitive," he retorted.

"Well, get over it. Me being ambitious doesn't mean I'm abandoning you," I said.

"We thought you were this bright kid with an academic future ahead of you. I've never told you this, but it was really hard for me to see you so upset after you dropped out of college," Mom confided.

"For two educated Jewish parents what I did was an unspeakable *shanda*. So you decided to emotionally abandon me and charge me rent, paying for my crimes in pennies?" I wasn't going to let her off so easily.

"I thought if you had a job you'd feel better about yourself. At night you would get drunk in your room. I'd go in and you'd weep on my shoulder and not want me to leave. You were like a baby. I tried to reach you, but—" Mom's voice caught in her throat.

"So when I was about to lose my mind you saw that as me failing?" I asked angrily.

"I wanted the perfect family. If you weren't getting scholarships and being a teetotaler like us I would have been disappointed," my father admitted. "And I was jealous of how close you were to your brother."

"But you always wanted us to be friends," Fury pointed out.

"I wanted all of us to love each other as a family, a quartet," Dad said sadly.

"We could have if you'd let us," I told him.

"You still can," Dr. Craig almost whispered.

As we headed toward the subway station, Fury paired up with Dad and I walked with Mom. Strolling through silent streets, I thought of all our family dinners, a ritual binding us together, our past meals punctuated by psychoanalysis and laughter. I suddenly hoped tuna casserole and Italian lemon chicken, old comforts, could sustain us into the future.

"Mom, about those nights when I cried. I know you wanted to help, but I don't think I wanted to be reached. I had to figure things out on my own. I love you." I hugged her. "Let's get some famous pizza."

Part III

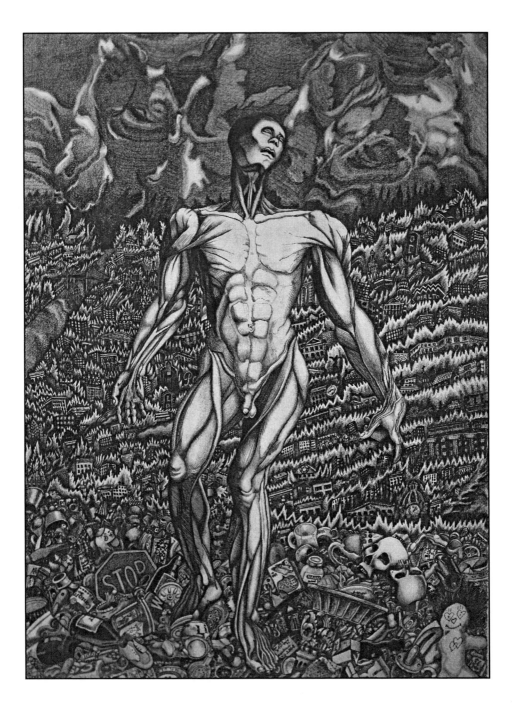

16
Ball Drops

"I haven't seen Grandpa Morris since my Bar Mitzvah. Why do we have to go to the Midwest now?" I asked over my Amtrak microwave beef-and-carrot dinner.

"I want you to see my father before he dies," Dad explained.

We were on a train speeding toward Springfield, Illinois, across America, past rundown industrial plants and brown rivers, two weeks before New Year's 2008. The lull of the train appeased my father's aerophobia but to me, the cramped shuttle train felt suffocating.

"I can't eat this," said Fury, pushing away a Caesar salad crusted with freezer burn.

I took a gulp of bitter merlot, staring out the train windows at my pale reflection. Dad had asked Mom to stay at home and take care of their basset hound, Rhonda, so we three boys could bond over saying good-bye.

At twenty-two, I had moved out of the ghetto to Ridgewood, the quiet border between Brooklyn and Queens. Just putting geography between myself and Chubbs had helped me quit my coke habit completely. As I left it behind, Bushwick, like the Lower East Side before it, succumbed to gentrification. Organic health food stores and coffee shops serving artisan baked goods opened. Old buildings covered in graffiti were torn down to make way for modern lofts where trust fund babies masquerading as starving artists quickly moved in. Hip bars with mixologists making infused cocktails catered to drunken young crowds under elevated train tracks.

Meanwhile, I had cofounded a small, start-up quarterly magazine in Brooklyn for which I had big hopes. I had finally harnessed my ambition. Instead of being a gallery- and club-hopping model/actor/lead singer/poet/fame shark, I had focused on words that really mattered to me. Once directed, my dreams stopped being self-destructive and vain and started being hard work. Helping others get published along with myself, pushing to get at painful parts of my past, and dealing with them on the page instead of snorting a line or having twenty drinks surprisingly suited me.

We weren't seeing Dr. Craig anymore. At our last session he had prescribed mandatory family dinners at least once a week. Every Thursday we met at a different restaurant, forced to talk to each other, healing over hot food—better than any session in Midwood. But now, just as I was looking forward to my future, the family past was dragging me thousands of miles back. Yet I hoped this emotional errand would finally heal my relationship with my father forever. If I found out for good exactly how Grandpa Morris had hurt him, I could more completely understand our own struggle.

Currency was clearly an issue between my dad and my grandfather. "He's lived so long, there's not much money left," Dad told us on the long train ride. "My mom died of a stroke when I was twenty-five. Morris remarried Belle nine months later. She made him promise he would never give any money to his son or grandchildren. And even after she died things stayed that way. Neither of you is even mentioned in his will."

"That's horrible. How could he agree to that?" Fury asked Dad.

"He grew up poor. His father baked bagels and never said a word to him. They were completely Old Country. When he could afford it, Morris became very concerned with his own comfort." Dad shrugged. "Right now, he's basically living for three hots and a cot."

"But what about his family's future?" I persisted.

"Look, he's selfish, but he'd still love to see you," he said.

Grandpa Morris's male nurse, Keith, picked us up at the train station in Springfield, Illinois. When we arrived at Morris's house he was sitting down to dinner. The house had nothing hanging on its bare beige walls. It was the exact opposite of the home my father had created and looked more like a motel than our room at the Comfort Inn. My grandfather was sitting in his kitchen, spoon-feeding himself chicken noodle soup, mashed potatoes, and canned corn.

"Hi, Dad!" my father chirped too cheerfully. "Look who's here."

Morris looked up blankly, then acknowledged us with apparent satisfaction. He recognized Fury and me right away and ignored his son.

🦋

"These are my grandsons," he croaked to the caretaker.

At ninety-four he was gaunt and bleary eyed, confined to a wheelchair and big leather recliner, which folded out mechanically by pressing a button on its plush arm. Dad and I both shared Morris' same lanky frame, but his was now drawn and wasted. I wondered if Dad would one day be like this—decrepit, wearing a beret. Would I have to take care of him then? I decided if I did, I would do it with compassion and warmth. I wasn't scared of old people or their complicated metal aids, but I noticed how expensive Grandpa Morris's geriatric devices looked. He had multiple stainless walkers, towers of medicine bottles, wheelchairs, bed pans, the best of the best.

"He got into a bunch of sugar cookies last week," Keith said, laughing. "Ate the whole package before I could stop him."

"Dad, you can't have any sugar. You're diabetic," my father reprimanded.

Morris looked up at us, smiling mischievously.

"Leave me alone. I'm fine." He slurped his soup.

"Dad, talk with your grandsons, Hazak and Yuvi," My father said loudly. He ushered us around the table and took the nurse into another room. A silence fell over the kitchen while my grandfather ate, looking in our general direction.

"Actually we changed our names to Fury and Royal," my brother informed him.

"Good soup," Morris nodded.

I noticed a *Reader's Digest* by his bowl.

"Do you like this magazine?" I asked, picking it up.

He nodded. I opened the magazine.

"Do you want me to read to you?"

I began to flip through, coming to an illustration of a beautiful young couple by a waterfall. The woman was in front of the man, holding his hand as if leading him somewhere fantastic. My grandfather stopped eating and stared at the scene. He reached with shaky hands. I let him hold it and look closer. He took his dirty napkin and clumsily marked the page, setting it back on the table.

"I want to go to bed," he announced.

"I guess you'll dream about this," I said, staring at the picture.

We spent most of the next day cautiously driving over icy roads to the three thrift shops in town. Sorting through and saving scraps of other people's lives was still one of my father's passions. I thought of him fleeing to New York in the '60s from this frozen conservative wasteland—an angry young artist in search of acclaim, defying his own father's disregard.

"This is the only interesting thing to do here," Dad said. "And I know you two don't want to spend every day cooped up with Grandpa Morris. Neither do I. At least he's not as bad as last time."

"What happened last time?" Fury asked.

"He kept trying to walk in on me while I was in the bath." Dad grimaced. "He also walked around naked. His body looked like mine. It shocked me."

"That's disgusting," Fury said.

As we drove along, an announcer on the car radio warned about treacherous road conditions. Highways were empty, affording a clear view of strip malls built like prison blocks. But thrift shopping was a love my brother and I now shared with our dad and this excursion proved worth the nasty trek. He showed us the best Salvation Army in town and we sorted through racks of clothes together.

"Ewww, look at these!" Dad laughed at a pile of ugly, wrinkled sweaters.

"Check it!" Fury unearthed a vintage Dior button up with sleeves a different color from the rest. Our bags crammed with cheap treasures, we then braved a reluctant descent back to reality, beginning with the greasy rotisserie chicken we picked up at Shnuck's supermarket for Grandpa Morris. When we got home, we made up plates and sat in front of his television watching *Tila Tequila: A Shot at Love* on MTV.

"Who is she?" Dad asked.

"She's famous for being the most viewed page on Myspace." I rolled my eyes.

"She's gorgeous," he said, glued to the screen.

"She looks like E.T. in drag," I said, pissed off that Dad was so immediately obsessed with a trashy celebrity who would do anything for fifteen seconds of immortality. A year ago, I would have been desperate to be a contestant on the show to escape my family. Now I knew I had to be there with my father to say good-bye to my grandfather. I never wanted my relationship with Dad to be as bad as theirs.

"This is stupid," Grandpa Morris announced, then fell asleep.

Keith, the caretaker, wanted to know all about New York.

"Do you speak Jewish there?" he asked.

"Judaism is a religion, not a language," my father answered, laughing. "I speak some Yiddish, but so does everyone in New York."

"Oh, sorry," Keith mumbled. "I have to go run Morris's bath."

Once the sleepy old man was in the bathtub, I cornered my father: "Why is Morris leaving all his money to his sisters-in-law and the one synagogue in this backward town instead of his own blood?"

"To buy his way into heaven," my father replied too quickly.

"More like a plaque on the back of a prayer bench," I muttered.

"I thought Jews don't believe in heaven," Fury said.

What dignity wouldn't the men in our family sacrifice in this quest for immortality? Instead of honoring their families and the close, unbreakable blood bonds that should have made them feel secure, they turned their dreamy gaze on distant acclaim and forged toward it, leaving a path of loneliness with every insistent footstep.

Perhaps it was then, as Keith shuttled Morris out of the bathroom, that I finally understood my father's courage: consciously or not, he had broken this pattern. He loved making art, and he was brilliant and dedicated. But early in the game he'd seen through the glitter of ambition, and recognized his wife and his children as lasting loves.

Fame is fleeting, dynamic and deadly. It turns talent slick and cleaves distance between artist and world. It's filled with false fixes; I felt so empty without fame that I sold my body to Evelyn. With no sense of deserving love, I auctioned myself to the next bidder—as if my affections weren't worth a damn. I shuddered at these memories of self-loathing. In the stale, climate-controlled air, I could still almost relate to Tila's desperation to be on TV, but not to her fake desire or those of her phony contestants.

Now back in our midst, Morris stealthily reached for the TV remote while we were distracted, apparently as disgusted with Tila's bisexual mind games as I was.

"But I'm watching this, Dad," my father scolded, moving the remote to the other side of the table where Morris couldn't reach it.

That night, Fury and I feverishly packed, eager to return to New York and our respective projects.

"When we get back, I'm going to direct a gangster rap music video," Fury said.

"Can I be rapping in it wearing my Tims?" I asked.

"Of course," he grinned.

Even though we had been in Illinois for only a few days, the dreary winter highways and the specter of Grandpa Morris's degeneration—coupled with his clear disdain for our father—made me hunger for our busy city obsessed with fast living.

Fury and I went outside of our Comfort Inn to smoke a final Marlboro Red. We made our way through a convention of fat truckers who had overtaken the lobby, armed with beers: Bleached blond, crew cut, ripped clothes, bottom of the gas tank. As we beelined for the exit we heard someone offer over the din: "I got five bucks for a blow job."

So outside of New York, stuck in this hick frozen place, I was scared for my brother and me. That trucker's words cut through me like Patrice's fingers so long ago. Evelyn had given me fifty dollars. But now, I laughed, ushering Fury quickly into the cold night. The frosty parking lot was packed with huge trucks, illuminated by the neon signs of Walmart, 7-Eleven, and a shop selling Christian paraphernalia.

"You know, you're eighteen, the same age I was when Evelyn ripped off my jean shorts and sucked my dick," I confessed, trying to sound blasé as I shared this painful moment of my past.

"I've never been with another guy. Why did you let him do that?" Fury asked.

"He wanted it." My teeth chattered.

"But what did you want?"

"My ticket to fame."

This answer didn't surprise my brother.

"Whatever the agenda, we should all fool around with someone of the same sex once. That makes you the most straight guy I know," Fury said.

"What?" I was used to my brother's eccentric analysis, but couldn't follow his logic.

"Now you know for sure what you don't want. You just found out the shitty way. Most guys are too scared. I'm sure a lot of them have lingering doubts," My brother hazarded.

I realized he was right, in that I harvested no lingering doubts. But my clarity had come at a cost: I had created a chaotic world around me that mimicked a warped inner mindscape. Drinking and drugs blurred boundaries. I had become involved with only men I didn't desire physically and only women I didn't trust emotionally. I had become a master at disassociation, telling myself I could never be loved.

The truth was, I was terrified to let anyone touch me at all.

Since childhood I had regarded sex as a shameful secret, a humiliation that disgusted me. I had let all the wrong people handle me, and now I feared no girl would want to hold my tainted skin to heal it. But I couldn't mend myself. I needed a woman's love.

Before going to the train station the next day we went to say goodbye to Morris. It would be the last time we'd see him. He was nodding off in his mechanical recliner.

"I'm tired, leave me alone." He waved his hands, shooing us away.

I left Morris's sparse house feeling sad for my father. He had made such an effort. He'd pursued social work as a way to understand and love his dad. I knew he had expected more closure from this trip. But I had finally learned the truth about what had hurt my father so deeply. Morris was dismissive and silent, a blank slate that made Dad strive to be more vibrant, filling canvases with bright brushstrokes. Dad was visibly shaken as we waited on the freezing train platform.

"I thought our good-bye would be different. You know, somehow I hoped he'd hug me at the end or something," he said, his eyes watering.

Fury and I hugged him as the train thundered into the station, its whistle sharp through the frosty air.

Two weeks later my Dad called to tell me Morris was dying.

"I thought we already went through this," I moaned to myself, after hanging up the phone. My father was getting back on Amtrak to return to Springfield. Fury, Mom, and I would follow, "only when a doctor pronounces him dead," I insisted. Grandpa Morris died five days later on December 29th. According to Jewish custom, the body had to be buried within forty-eight hours. I was livid, thinking it just like Grandpa Morris to ruin my New Year's Eve plans.

Back in the Midwest, Dad met us at the station, and we picked up pizza on the way to Morris's house.

"I'm obsessed with Tila Tequila. I watch it all day. She's so awful, but I can't stop," Dad said as we crawled over icy roads. I was uncomfortable knowing we would be sleeping steps away from my grandfather's deathbed.

"Isn't it a little strange staying there?" Mom asked.

"Why spend money, when we have perfectly good accommodations?" Dad asked.

"Because it's a death house," Fury replied.

"Let's put on the radio," Dad said, and tried to smile from behind the wheel of Grandpa Morris's Chrysler. "Wouldn't that be nice?"

After dinner later that evening, we rummaged through Morris's possessions, intent on taking away whatever we could in the absence of his love—and before Belle's family could claim these remnants of my grandfather as well. On my 6-foot, 2-inch frame, all of Grandpa Morris's clothes were too small, but they fit Fury perfectly.

"That's a beautiful suit on you," Dad marveled, as Fury modeled it.

"His tuxedos are mine," Fury said.

I jealously searched Grandpa Morris's drawers for something I could keep. I found a framed black-and-white photo of Morris's fraternity on a dresser. My grandfather looked handsome and distinguished, his sleepy blue eyes distinguishing him from the rest of the men, like a movie star. In the dresser was a beautiful pair of brown leather dress shoes.

"Yes, these are my size," I said. I tried them on. "I can wear them to the funeral."

"Look, my paintings! He kept them," my father called, waving us over to a hall closet and pointing at some of his early work, covered in dust. Here were the buildings and people of the Lower East Side in the '60s and '70s, rough tenements and tough faces rendered richly by my father's hand—history hiding in this closet in the Midwest. Each piece had been carefully preserved in bubble wrap.

"I gave Morris these as wedding gifts when he remarried that bitch Belle," Dad said. "She must have stored them in here. Well, they're mine again." Dad grinned as he reclaimed his lost canvases protectively. I loved seeing Dad so happy salvaging his relics, yet knew Morris had stowed them there out of shame, so no one in his closed-off community could see his son's lively and risqué creations.

"Oh, I almost forgot. He left something special for you guys," my father said.

"Is it money?" Fury asked.

"Yeah, sort of." Dad pulled a small package carefully wrapped in white tissue paper from Grandpa Morris's nightstand.

I eagerly tore the tissue away, revealing two silver dollars from 1885, a hundred years before I was born, still perfectly polished.

"That's the small fortune he left you," Dad explained. "I looked up their value. They are worth about thirty dollars apiece."

The next day we met with Morris's rabbi and his in-laws. Even after Belle's death five years before, her remaining sisters had stubbornly kept power of attorney over my grandfather, guarding their investment with zeal, considering they were ninety and eighty-six years old. Annette and Sarah also had mechanical recliners they never moved from. I tried desperately to think of something positive I could say, something that might open their hearts—and their pockets filled with my grandfather's money.

"He was a quietly courageous man," I volunteered, referring to Grandpa Morris's service in WWII.

"I remember him visiting New York and staying at the Hilton Hotel on Sixth Avenue. He took us shopping at FAO Schwartz and had the fattest roll of fifty dollar bills I'd ever seen," Fury said.

When my line made it into the rabbi's speech the next day at the funeral home, I was proud. As the rabbi orated, I learned information about my grandfather's times that I had never known while he was living. Morris's earliest memory had been neighbors on his Cincinnati street joyously burning an effigy of Kaiser Wilhelm. His own father, who worked from sunrise making bagels and bialys, never spoke to him. He was the baby of five siblings and was a dreamy Momma's Boy who never did well in school. He lied to his fiancée who became my dad's mom that he owned a soda company that he didn't really. Maybe that's why she hated my dad so much and told him he was ugly—he was the product of his father's lie.

Fury and I shook hands with octogenarian guests all carrying walkers and canes. The funeral parlor was packed; it seemed the whole town knew Morris. I realized my grandfather had been popular with everyone except his family. The reception area was covered in overstuffed couches and cheap paintings of fruit.

"Do you want to view the body?" the rabbi asked.

Fury and I adamantly shook our heads, "No."

"I'm okay," Dad said as Mom gripped his hand.

"We'd like to," said his ninety-year-old sister-in-law

I sat quietly in the front row as the casket was wheeled out into a waiting hearse. My family piled into Grandpa Morris's Chrysler and drove to the cemetery.

"Isn't it funny," Dad said, "that an immigrant Jew will be buried in the same cemetery as Abraham Lincoln? Grandpa Morris would have loved that. He always had a taste for fame."

"He would have liked the glory of it," Mom agreed.

"What do you mean? I never knew Morris wanted to be famous!" I shouted.

"Oh yeah, my dad had all these cockamamie fantasies about being a tall, handsome movie star. He was an egomaniac, always looking for a way to break big," Dad said. "After Morris had spinal surgery ten years ago, he wrote a letter to the head of HarperCollins about publishing his book of dirty jokes. It was probably an aftereffect of the anesthesia that discombobulated him."

I grinned at the gray sky out my car window. It was incredible to think my desperation for fame might have been genetic. Generations of Jewish immigrant men in my family had sought acclaim to prove themselves worthy of this modern American Dream.

A freezing wind whipped up as we took our seats under a small tent in front of the deep grave. An employee began to lower the casket, which bumped against the sides.

"Oopsy daisy," Dad muttered.

Mom burst out laughing and had to bury her face in her faux leopard coat. The employee looked bored with the routine. The rabbi chanted the *Kadish* prayer for the dead as we all shivered, then one by one the group, all dressed in black, went up to shovel dirt on the coffin. I threw the earth on quickly, watching as the gold placard on his coffin was covered: MORRIS BROZGOLD 1913 - 2007.

🦋

Later there was a brief and small meal at his in-laws'—egg salad in large plastic bowls.

"Death and mayonnaise," Fury said in my ear.

As snow piled steadily my family drove to our New Year's Eve dinner. The restaurant was festooned with streamers and bright balloons. After leaving a gravesite and a house full of grieving guests, it felt strange to be surrounded by such festivity, a celebration of resolutions that my grandfather had left his son and grandsons to make in his stead.

"Well, the show must go on," Dad said as we were seated.

I froze, half-buttered roll in hand. This motto had haunted my childhood, making me feel that no matter what pain or loss I felt, I must smile wider. Perform and it would pass. Now I related to it differently, seeing sadly its tired wisdom.

"I'm just glad it's over," Dad said, digging into his roast chicken giddily when it came.

"Can I order wine?" Fury asked.

"Sure," Mom said.

I was surprised she would allow him to drink underage, even more shocked when both my strictly sober parents ordered glasses of merlot.

"To you—I love you all," Dad said, his eyes wet.

"To family," I added.

"*L'Chaim*, to life," Mom said.

"To Grandpa Morris," Fury put in, as we clinked.

"I can't wait to get back to New York." Dad suddenly laughed.

"Me neither." I smiled over the rim of my glass.

"We'll all be back home together soon," Mom said.

Later, with my parents in bed early, Fury and I tried to watch the ball drop in Times Square on my grandfather's prized possession: his 65-inch TV.

"It's so depressing to watch tourists celebrating in our city," Fury said.

"You're right," I agreed. "Let's change it."

We flipped through channels, settling on porn star Jenna Jameson's *E! True Hollywood Story*. An old part of me related to her quest for fame by any means possible. But after a family funeral on New Year's, I felt content to be sitting safely next to Fury on a cozy couch with Mom and Dad snoring in the next room. Bizarrely, I thought that even if I wasn't a celebrity, I had so far lived a famous life. I had drunk my way to a DUI, been photographed on the street, sold my body for film roles, lived like the scrappy downtown art stars of Warhol's day. It seemed that a prerequisite for being a celebrity was being an asshole.

Even more strangely, it also seemed that all Americans were celebrities, the culture of fame now the language of our world. We were all lonely and desperate for adulation in some way. We understood what it was to be adored and to want so much that it would come to crush us. Myspace had long become an Internet ghost town full of cyber tumbleweeds, but now our Facebook friends were our fans, and our profile photos were paparazzi shots, immortalizing private occasions and raising them on the pedestal of public forum. We did not stop to cherish moments; instead, we sought to express them in the form of a press release, as if this gave added importance to the tangled tangents of our lives. As if in witnessing each other's every milestone they would become bigger than we are. And maybe they did.

When Dad drove Mom, Fury, and me to the train station the next day, it was still snowing. We were catching a train to O'Hare, then flying back to New York while Dad stayed behind and sorted out the antique china his mother had collected and packed in crates in Morris's basement. Losing Grandpa Morris seemed to liberate Dad. I watched him laughing with Fury and Mom inside the waiting room while I smoked a Marlboro Red on the deserted train platform, which was crusted with a thin sheet of ice. My father caught my eye and excused himself, coming out of the warm station and slipping. I caught his arm before he fell.

"Thank you for coming. This hasn't been easy for me." His words came out in puffs.

I was sad he had never been close with his father, had moved halfway across the country to get away from him. I wanted to let my father know that I understood him now. I had always loved him. Nine hundred twenty-one miles from home there came a reunion. Over was my father's father's life. Behind me was my hunger for synthetic fruit. If fame forced me to outdo myself, love expected me to improve. I threw my arms around Dad's shoulders, squeezing past the down winter coat I knew he'd rescued from the trash.

"Thanks for taking me with you," I said.

Hebrew and Yiddish Glossary

The words as I, Royal Young, understand them:

Alte Old, older or great, as in *alte bubbi*, or greatgrandmother.

Babcha, Bubbeleh (Bubbi) Jewish terms for "grandmother." I call mine Babbi, a sort of adaptation.

Babushka A scarf, which is worn wrapped around the head.

Bar mitzvah The ceremony that is held when a Jewish boy comes of age (13 years old) as a man; a *Bat Mitzvah* is for girls of 12 or 13.

Bimah The raised platform or stage in a synagogue.

Drek Garbage, crap.

Fakakta Nonsense, ridiculous, a person or set of ideas that make no sense. Also: dirty, shitty, full of crap.

Folksbiene The Yiddish theatre.

Gefayrlich Fated or thick-headed. A person who has his or her own agenda and is going to do whatever they want.

Goyishe Anything or anyone non-Jewish.

Kadish The Hebrew prayer for the dead.

Kosher (glatt) Religious rules governing what observant Jews can and cannot eat. I adore bacon too much to ever have followed them.

Nogoodnick Someone who is up to no good; suspicious character.

Pisher A person of no consequence or importance.

Schmata A rag.

Schul A Jewish house of worship, a synagogue or temple.

Shabbos Sabbath.

Shanda An unforgivable sin.

Shiksa A non-Jewish woman. I've always been attracted to shiksas.

Shtetl A small, Jewish town or village. Usually poor, and usually in Eastern Europe.

Tallis A ceremonial Jewish prayer shawl.

Traif The opposite of Kosher food.

Yalmuke A ceremonial Jewish head cap.

Zaftig Curvy, voluptuous, heavy, "Rubensesque."

Zayde Jewish term for "grandfather."

Acknowledgments

This is only one version of my life story. Though much of this book is about understanding our struggles, my parents have been such an endlessly supportive, caring, strong, loving and solid presence in my life. Thank you to my beautiful Mamacita and Dad. To my Babbi and Zayde, who believed in my future when others didn't, taught me how to fight for my dreams and mostly, how to love toughly, with everything. My brother who helps me be wiser and who I couldn't live without.

Naomi Rosenblatt, a perfect publisher who can peer into the future. Susan Shapiro, my writing mentor who channeled and honed my ambition. Again, to my father whose incredible, startling, powerful images are included in this book. His artwork always helped me make sense of the world: sometimes dangerous and beautiful, but always safe when rendered by his brushstrokes. And to my dear friend Amanda Segur, whose vibrant photographs capture the Lower East Side we explored and lost together. You taught me about young love, and also about how to pose.

All the amazing editors, writers, readers, fans, lovers, haters, friends who helped and inspired me along the way: ACE, Carlo Alcantara, Joe Antol, Stacey Ashton, Stephen Bach, Corinna Barsan, Marie-Helene Bertino, Jim Beam, Lori Bizzoco, Stella Bouzakis, David Bowie, J Butta, Blanche, Mike Brazilier, Jennifer Caeser, Kristin Cecelia, 50 Cent, Greg Chan, Leopoldine Core, Nicole and Isiah Contes, Hilary Davidson, Maj Anya DeBear, Lisa Dierbeck, Kristin Dwyer, Erik Erikson, Alice Feiring, Fiddy, Alison Fleminger, Shani Friedman, Ron Galella, Brooke Geahan, Alyson Gerber, Mel Gibson, Brian Goodwin, Victoria Grantham, Myles Grovosky, Erasmo Guerra, Dorian Hamilton, Gregory Henry, Dwayne Jahn, Kristen Johnston, Dave Jones, Kastoory Kazi, Prianka Kazi, Jayme Keith, Diana Kinscherf, Amy Klein, Miles Klee, Angela Ledgerwood, Julian Levine, Jesse Levitt, Francis Levy, Lisa Lewis, Ed Litvak, Matt, The M sisters (truly my muses), Alex Marinacci, Naja Matthews, Paige McGreevy, Royce Meier, Nicholas Milanoff, Vica Miller, Graham Mooney, Lauren Mooney, Morrissey, Jeannine Oppewall, Patrice Dickerson Neals, Tony O'Neil, Sasha Panyuta, Jeanine Pepler, Rich Prior, Alexander Pridgen, Jerry Portwood, Tony Powell, Sarah Reidy, Traven Rice, Paul Richert, Rhonda, Penina Roth, Sarah Showfety, Michael Signorelli, Lucy Silberman, Evan Silverman, G. Singer, Sharan Singh, Devan Sipher, Jennifer Sky, Ely Spivack, Alina Smirnova, Jerry Stahl, Jonathan Stein, Lianne Stokes, Gem Stone, Jennifer Strom, Wendy Sylvester, Nancy Sylvor, Alexandria Symonds, Sylvain Sylvain, Jennifer Tang, Barbara Utendahl, Simon Van Booy, Jeanine O'Brien Waldron, Kate Walter, Andy Wang, Leah Wells, Matt Wise, Sophie Wise, Kera Yonker, Coco Young, Katie Zaun.

About the Author

Royal Young was born and bred on New York's Lower East Side. *Fame Shark* is his debut memoir. Young's writing has been featured in *Interview Magazine*, the *New York Post, The Lo Down, Vol. 1 Brooklyn, BOMB Magazine, The Believer, The Villager, Jewcy, The Forward, 3:AM Magazine, Mr. Beller's Neighborhood, New York Press, Downtown Express*, and *The Rumpus* among others.